NATURAL URGES

ChrisTina Leimer

SEATTLE, WASHINGTON

Natural Urges is available at discounts for purchases of 10 or more copies. For information, send an e-mail to info@twistedtreepress.com.

The names and identifying characteristics of persons in this book have been changed to preserve their privacy.

COPYRIGHT © 2002 by ChrisTina Leimer
Book Design by Kathryn E. Campbell
Editors: Susan Browne and Juliann Lowery
Author Photo by Lee Rodriguez

All rights reserved. This book, or parts thereof, may not be reproduced in any form without written permission of the author.

First edition paperback printed January 2003
ISBN: 0-9717950-0-2

Excerpt from "The Power of Perception" reprinted by permission of DeVorss Publications.
The Power of Perception by Marcus Bach
ISBN: 0875165230 DeVorss Publications: www.devorss.com

Natural Urges published by:

P.O. Box 17816
Seattle, WA 98107
www.twistedtreepress.com
info@twistedtreepress.com

Evidently there is a divine current of some kind ready to carry us through certain phases of life, and the more we realize this and give ourselves over to it, the better off we are. Yet who has the courage to believe it, the daring to expect it, the wisdom to understand it, or the prudence to conform to it?

Marcus Bach
The Power of Perception

This book is dedicated to
courage, daring, wisdom and prudence.

CONTENTS

Author's Introduction / 9

Reconnecting / 17

TURNING THE CULTURAL TIDE

Got My Own Spirituality / 29

Nature's Power / 35

The Positive Side of Violence / 39

Redefining Existence / 43

The Cenotaph Mirror / 47

ALL THAT WE ARE

Shifting Gears / 57

Beyond the Skin / 63

Powerful Thoughts / 67

Energy Exchanges / 73

Can We Choose? / 79

Hidden Talents / 85

THE WORLD IS MORE THAN WE KNOW

Between Two Worlds / 93

Killing Time / 97

We Are Not Alone / 99

Here, There or Everywhere? / 103

LIVING FROM SPIRIT

Riding the Waves / 111

Ways of Knowing / 115

Discovering Meaning / 119

Clear as a Crystal Bell / 123

Why Know? / 127

Main Attractions / 135

Seeing Patterns / 141

Making Connections / 145

Nocturnal Tuning / 149

Feet on the Ground / 155

AUTHOR'S INTRODUCTION

WE ALL HAVE A NATURAL URGE to know the secrets of the universe, to understand the mystery and meaning of life. To live in the flow, in the awe and wonder of our world. Too often, these natural urges we're born with recede as we grow up and learn to make our way through the world. We forget our experience of how alive the world is, of how we delight in simple things, unexpected things. "Practical" matters take precedence. As adults, we must take charge, set goals, and come up with a plan for our life. We must earn a living, raise our children, get an education, establish a career, then eventually, perhaps when we retire, we'll return to exploring this inkling that there's magic in our world. If our spark isn't extinguished by then.

This feeling of wonder, of mystery, is our spirit's voice, its way of letting us know that it exists, that life is more than physical bodies and chemical actions. Nothing is more practical, more pragmatic, than remembering and learning to follow the knowledge of the spirit we were born with. Our spirit knows where we came from and where we will go when we leave this world. It knows why we're here and how to navigate in both the spiritual and physical worlds. If we allow it, our spirit will guide us on our journey. If we refuse, we travel alone, without a compass or a map, stumbling and crashing, blindly making what we hope are corrections or steadily steering along a perhaps smooth, but meaningless road.

I refer to the practice of following our spirit's guidance as "natural spirituality." I think of it as "natural" because insights spring directly from our own spiritual experiences, and often from the natural world. By spirituality I mean simply, of the spirit—the core, the life force, the essence of who we are, our power source. It connects us to all life and allows us to transcend the boundaries of our own skin and ego. Natural spirituality is not the province of any one of us, not the domain of a special few. Spirit is in each of us. We can deny its existence and ignore it, or allow it to open us to the mystery and revelations in even the mundane processes of daily life.

My spirit has never allowed me to ignore it. I've tried. Especially when it wanted me to face realities I didn't want to see. Or when it badgered me to make decisions that required personal sacrifice. In other words, when I couldn't just do what I wanted to do or take the easy way out.

There have been times when I couldn't feel my spirit's presence.

When suddenly, I seemed to be alone. These were testing periods so I could find out if I truly learned, if I was willing and able to apply my spiritual knowledge to my actions in the physical world. Had I gained wisdom?

Sometimes, when I'm not getting the message or I'm too far off my path, my spirit insists that I pay attention and change course. It gets as loud as it needs to. If I ignore a nudge, my inner guide shoves me. If I stay on my feet but refuse to sidestep, it may pull a curtain down or shut a door, making it impossible for me to continue determinedly marching in the same direction. That's how my spirit got me to write this book.

For as long as I can remember, I've kept my connection to the spiritual world to myself. I've spoken about it with only my closest friends, yet even then I left out some of the experiences I believed they'd never understand or accept. I was trying to protect myself from derision, from being dismissed, or considered deluded, out of touch with "the real world."

Not only did I believe people might hurt me, I believed spiritual truths are precious and fragile and so can be damaged as well. Spirituality is the driving force in my life. It's my solace, my joy, my strength, and my guide. My respect and reverence for the spiritual process and its revelations was so intense that I didn't want to share my awareness and run the risk that others would destroy these workings and truths, distort or pervert them, or use them in some self-serving way, and in the process, maybe destroy me too. I wanted to protect the sacred knowledge and keep my life on an even keel. To do that, I believed I had to keep my spirituality to myself.

I resisted too because I doubted that what I knew was real, that my spiritual experiences were anything beyond the workings of a mind that spent too much time inside itself. I'm a scientist from the "Show Me" state. I was born asking "why" and "how do you know." I want to see evidence and hold reality in my hand. I want data, testing and logic. I want proof. Even when I get proof, I want to test it just one more time before I believe it. My childhood Sunday school teachers, exasperated with my questioning, sat me in the hall. Faith, they told me, is simply to be accepted, not scrutinized.

Yet, with my inquisitive, analytical nature, I couldn't help but question. The Bible stories and tenets didn't match my deepest sense of spiritual knowing or spark the elation of connectedness with all life that I felt in the woods, fields and creeks and occasionally in church. Nor did these tenets correspond with my observations of the world. Little else in my external environment validated my inner nature or experiences either. So, I doubted that I knew what I know.

Doubts and fears poisoned clear communication with my spirit. That poison produced beliefs that were in direct contradiction to my spiritual wisdom. Truth is to be shared, not hoarded. And it doesn't need my protection. Spiritual truths can stand on their own, shining beneath the mud, always available to seekers who are willing to dig. As for protecting myself, I can't live in fear. I can no longer push back such a crucial, vital part of who I am and my reason for being.

Accepting and trusting my spirit's guidance brings me inner peace and a strong sense that life is proceeding as it should.

I've known for most of my adult years that my purpose involves communicating about spiritual matters, but I've been reluctant to accept that mantle. Fifteen years ago, I wrote a book about spiritual consciousness but when a publisher expressed interest, I backed off. I put the manuscript away and never looked at it again. I don't know where it is, or if it even still exists.

Nearly two years ago, my spirit forced me to return to my calling by shutting down my desire to read and ability to comprehend. I grew irritated with conversations and media voices, just didn't want to hear them. I had difficulty swallowing food without choking. I couldn't drink without water running down my chin or coughing. The theme, the message in this experiential metaphor, was that I'd taken in as much as I could or should. Now it was time to put things out, to express, to give my insights to others.

My ego produces the doubt and fear that cages me. When I send this jailer away, I can stand on my own, strong in my spirit's guidance, secure in the knowledge that I'm doing what I was born to do, and free to let my spirit sing.

I know I'm not alone. Many of us today have a long history of being attacked for trying to bring truth to the world. We remember these experiences, usually unconsciously, and respond to our fear. But now human consciousness is on the cusp of change. A critical mass of people are ready for transformation, longing to understand the glimmers they're experiencing, poised to evolve and grow spiritually. Many facilitators, in various roles, are receiving a call to remember and sharpen their talents and many have been off the starting block for years to help this personal-social-cultural transformation take place.

This book is one of those means of facilitation.

Natural Urges is about listening to our spirit's voice, about finding and following our internal compass, about the natural energy processes underlying daily life that our spirit is aware of but our logical minds may never be able to explain. It's about aligning ourselves with the natural energy systems of our planet and the universe to transform our lives and our world.

Opening to our spirit's guidance is not a religious practice; it's just a natural part of life we've been cut off from by Western culture. Natural spirituality is not a system of rights and wrongs, or rules to follow. We've outlived externally imposed, dogmatic systems and now must develop and rely on internal guidance and awareness.

The world we've created is highly complex. With so many new dilemmas and so much information, black and white thinking and decisions are no longer effective. We must be open to the subtleties of each situation and its circumstances. To know and follow the right direction in complicated, ambiguous conditions, we must be able to act from spirit, not from ego. When we determine and take the right direction, the congruence between our inner and outer selves will reveal new insights, unfold deeper layers of existence, and give us a calm assurance that we are traveling our path.

I've written *Natural Urges* in a conversational style, using essays and stories that both show the natural spirituality process at work and the insights, questions and quandaries listening to my spirit has raised. I chose this style because following our spirit's guidance is a personal process of risk, discovery, and unfolding. We can benefit from others' experience, and see common characteristics of the process, but ultimately we must sense and understand our own spirit's rhythm, pace, and language.

Direct experience and reflection are key. So is sharing experiences, questions, and insights. "Ah-ha moments," when we recognize our experience in the experience of others, can help stimulate awakening, deepen our connection to spirit, let us see our own experiences in a new light, and show us that we are not alone. I hope *Natural Urges* will be such a catalyst.

RECONNECTING

OUR SPIRIT IS OUR GUIDE and companion in this world. It's natural for us to be in direct, constant contact with it. It's the source of our strength and our connection to all life. Our spirit is our anchor in the physical world, the cord that connects us to the dynamic forces of the unseen realms. Without it we have no power, no substance, nothing that will withstand the trials of physical existence.

The yearnings we feel—to be all that we are, to grow, to know our place in the world and our purpose in life, to find substance, meaning and value in living, and to experience the mystery and wonder of our universe—are natural urges, the desires of the spirit. When we're guided by spirit, these urges are fulfilled. There's no striving for them, no frustration and anxiety, no despair or longing. Instead, there's gratitude, joy, strength, confidence, courage and love. There is a solid foundation on which to stand, a warm place that soothes the pains of life. There is depth and breadth and dimension to all that we see and experience. The complexities of life are taken as they come, neither feared nor pursued. They are experienced with all of the richness they possess.

This is the natural state of the human spirit. But we have lost touch with it.

The physical world is a tough place to live without our natural power source. When we're born, we know that our spirit is our guide. We are our spirit, and we are the universal spirit. We know we are not separate and that all the energy of the universe can be called on to help us navigate the physical world. But soon we start to forget.

The physical world is a world of duality, of separation and segmentation that begins at birth. No longer connected to our mother's body, we must learn to operate our own, a completely different state of existence than in the spiritual world. Our senses are flooded with sights, sounds, textures, smells, tastes, and movement. We can get overwhelmed or preoccupied with the physical stimuli. We begin to disconnect from the unseen world and its presence within us fades from awareness. It's as if we're developing amnesia, being split apart, or abandoned. Ever wonder why young infants cry so much as the sun goes down?

If we make it through that stage still aware of our spirit, then it can start to fade once we begin to speak about it. Few Western adults will take seriously children's statements about invisible beings, foreknowledge of events to come, or messages from another world.

Those who do may call it imagination, and give the child direct or subtle messages to grow out of it. Eventually, we do. Or we keep it to ourselves while we quietly search for reasonable explanations or learn to doubt our sanity.

We also lose touch with parts of who we really are. The spiritual world contains no categories, but on the earth plane we are either a boy or a girl, and that determines a lot about how we're treated, what people will expect from us and what they will allow. We possess all of our body parts in the correct places and scale, or we don't. That differentiates us and influences our life course. The color of our skin or the language or bank balance of our parents sets us apart and puts us on a unique path of collective and personal experiences.

We even learn to split ourselves. The nature of culture is that collective ideas and values become part of us without our even realizing or questioning it. So we learn to do and be only what is acceptable. We forget or suppress other parts of who we are. Then we absorb other cultural values, like the importance of winning or fear of making a mistake, and so we start to do only the things we're good at, sports or music or painting or math or.... People start putting us in little boxes too. We're the smart one, or the sweet one, or the stubborn one. So contrary or unique traits fall away, or drop out of our consciousness, and we strive to match the labels, or chafe at having to.

No wonder so many of us feel like we don't belong in this world, and why we try to escape it. Our children are killing themselves and each other at increasing rates and at younger ages. More and more of our elderly are opting out early. Escape or numbing attempts like drug and alcohol addictions are widespread. Even the quest for spiritual awareness can turn into absorption in spiritual ecstasy and retreat from the world.

Living in the physical realm is not supposed to be a prison sentence. Earthly pleasures can be enjoyed in no other realm. Nor can the unique spiritual lessons of the physical world be learned anywhere else. But our spirit is supposed to be our companion, a living part of us that eases this leg of our journey and keeps us aware of the broader workings of life.

We can see this wholeness periodically, and feel it in ourselves occasionally, which is why we haven't given up hope, why we can still feel these natural urges. We can still see glimmers of who we are. But the human systems we've created, our social and cultural systems, have squelched and nearly eradicated our connection to our spirit, our awareness of our nature, our source of power and purpose. Humans are capable of creating their own environment, even of altering the natural world, and yet the environment we've created is antithetical to our nature. Why? Why would we make life harder than it needs to be? Why would we slowly strangle ourselves?

Severed from our spirit, we do not understand our nature, the nature of the earth, or the natural energy systems of life. We mistake the physical world and our physical selves as the totality of the natural order and construct our systems around that illusion.

A basic principle of the universe is that everything is energy, including our spirit. Energy is dynamic. That's its nature, our nature. We want to experience the world, to explore it, to marvel at it, to question it, to create it, to bring it into ourselves and put ourselves into it. We want to grow and be fulfilled. When we try to deny that nature, to run from it, squelch it or fail to nurture it in others, the trouble begins. This spirit smashing and neglect is the root of most social and psychological problems. Its effects are so devastating that they flood out beyond humanity and chew up the natural and supernatural worlds. Repressing this energy throws life out of balance and cuts us off from our own nourishment.

No wonder we thirst for substance, realness, and truth. No wonder we sense that there is more to life than we know. To quench our thirst, we will have to reconnect to our spirit, learn to move with it, and allow it to open us to the natural energy processes that are the underpinnings and workings of life.

Learning to live from our core, from our spirit, is an awakening in which we start remembering who we are, why we're here on this earth at this point in time, and what resources we have to bring to our task. For some, it will require learning the ways of the universe. For others, it will require remembering the knowledge they already possess but are keeping within.

Many of us are waking up, feeling a tug or a call. Maybe we haven't understood what it is yet or realized what direction or action we should take to respond, if any. There are many ways to clarity, many ways of knowing. That's one of the lessons of the universe and a basic tenet of the emerging consciousness.

Waking up to one's spirit can be subtle or jarring, gradual or sudden, a single event or a series of experiences. Some people experience a big event, an event they can't miss, one that jolts them and is so far out of their ordinary experience or belief system that they are compelled to search for its meaning. Their spirit is intent on waking them up and doing it immediately. Or maybe they've been ignoring subtler promptings for too long. Others may become increasingly uncomfortable with the way they're living, with their job or profession, with the part of the world they live in, with relationships. Or they may sense that there's something for them to do but they can't figure out what that something is.

Waking up and reconnecting to spirit is essential in expanding consciousness, our own, that of the planet and all life. We will learn to live in the world from a base of wisdom, wisdom that knows our purpose and our place, that is aware of the boundaries, limits and needs of the physical world, that understands non-physical forms of communication, that can teach us new ways to navigate the increasing complexities of life with understanding and acceptance.

This expanded consciousness cannot thrive within the old ways. It requires new paradigms, structures and methods of organization. We will need to redefine commonly accepted terms, dismantle and rebuild old structures and foundations, and develop new ways of understanding and living in the world that are congruent with the natural energy systems of our planet and the universe.

This change is not a matter of old wine in new bottles. It's not an era or state of existence we're reviving or returning to. It's not a resurrection of the world that is now passing, nor of ancient worlds of utopian lore. It's a new day. This transformation is our opportunity to consciously shape and build a more sustainable, natural, life-supporting world. It won't be utopian, as in all problems fixed, suffering eliminated, and humans and other animals frolicking gleefully together in lush, friendly forests where the trees bid us "good day" and there's free chocolate ice cream for everyone. Some things are inherent to physical existence, like the vagaries of the body, life cycles and learning, that often involve pain and sorrow. We can never completely eliminate these heartaches, but we shouldn't stop trying either. There's much to be learned in the trying.

Turning

the

Cultural Tide

In graduate school, nine years ago, I studied death and dying. I didn't intend to. My interest was in social change, specifically, how systems and cultures change when little or no organized push for change exists. When I saw that Americans were, in rapidly increasing percentages, beginning to cremate, rather than bury their dead, I knew that foundational forces must be shifting. Otherwise, we would never let go of such a widespread, emotionally charged, centuries old tradition as earth burial. Especially not in favor of replacing it with a practice most Western religions have considered pagan, punitive, or at the least, disrespectful.

As I read, researched, and reflected in order to understand this major cultural change, I began looking at life in the light of death. Through this lens, I could clearly see what makes me feel most alive. Trivial matters consumed less of my attention and energy. Extraneous issues melted away, revealing my core, the essence of who I am. I was undergoing a deeper transformation than earning a degree or developing a new career. Metaphorically, I was dying, with only inklings of what my rebirth would bring.

I felt a growing sense that my study was both literal and symbolic, both personal and cultural—as if the world and I were experiencing a dual and parallel transformation. Beneath the turbulent crosscurrents of contemporary cultures, I sensed a subtle pulse in the world, an underlying heartbeat undetectable with a stethoscope or microscope. The world, it appears, is dying too. But its seeds of rebirth are germinating, and I began to see their sprouting. These nascent social changes are the faint pulse that can be heard in silence, and felt in our core. They thrive beneath the tumultuous dominant trends, waiting, gestating. When they are born, when their pent-up power erupts, they will change the world.

GOT MY OWN SPIRITUALITY

THE FIRST TIME I SAID out loud in public, at a publisher's meeting, that I'm writing about spirituality, I got silence and confused looks. The response isn't much different if I say it one-on-one. *Uh, excuse me but I just remembered I'm late for an appointment,* or *How about those Mariners.* Sometimes I fix the awkwardness by switching the subject myself. Occasionally someone will ask what I mean, and maybe, eventually, test my openness with a spirituality story of their own.

Apparently clergy get this reaction too, when they reveal their vocation in secular settings. So what's the deal? Why is spirituality an uncomfortable subject?

One reason is that most people don't want to be harangued or get into any "you believe, I believe" arguments. Me either. When it comes to religion and politics, zeal and dogma hammer reason, discussion and dissenting opinion. We've seen the battles. We're wary.

Why wrinkle an otherwise acceptable day.

Secondly, most of the people I meet are educated laypersons. Indoctrinated with the supremacy of the intellect, rationality and the scientific method, we're not supposed to believe in the unseen, in spiritual powers or in God. Science is our religion. So earnestly discussing something as intangible, illusive and fantastic as spirituality can be embarrassing or nonsensical.

Then there's the big question: what are we talking about? What does spirituality mean? That term covers a lot of rocky ground these days, fraught with pits and boulders. Some people think I mean Christianity. Some assume New Age—another broad and amorphous term. Some equate it with spiritualism, a word usually associated with contacting the dead.

One way I've noticed that even people who are interested in spirituality shut down a potential conversation about it is by saying, "I've got my own spirituality." By that they usually mean, as I do, a set of ideas, guidelines, beliefs, and intuitions that guide us and help us make sense of our life. And they don't want to discuss those beliefs or try to explain them to anyone. Fair enough. In the U.S., we're free to think what we want to think, believe what we want to believe, and discuss what we want to discuss. The one hitch to discussing is that you need someone else to do it with. Otherwise you end up standing in a corner talking to yourself.

I want to discuss spirituality. Not argue about it, just exchange ideas and views. I don't really care what other people believe, as long as they don't act on some belief that tells them they have a right or a duty to hurt me or anyone else. My interest is in how we come to believe what we do, what questions we ask of ourselves and the world, what observations and experiences inform our beliefs about existence, and how these beliefs and values manifest in our daily lives.

For me, spirituality means simply "of the spirit" or the soul. It's our core, our essence, our power source, our internal compass or guide that plugs us in to all life and allows us to transcend our own ego and circumstances. Spirituality doesn't equate with religion and need not be associated with any traditional belief system, though it can and does co-exist. Spiritual guidance is in each of us—as natural as breathing, talking and walking. All we need do is be aware of it and go where our spirit leads us.

This definition is the essence of my own spirituality. I never could fit my spirituality into one of the religion or philosophy boxes. I explored the gamut of belief systems, from a multi-denominational Christian upbringing, to atheism, agnosticism, Taoism, Buddhism, New Age, secular humanism, transcendentalism, Scientology, psychology, mythology, and goddess and earth-centered religions. Their common themes intrigued me, and I found messages that rang true, but always something was missing or felt wrong, awkward, off the mark somehow. I couldn't buy the whole set.

Neither can most of us who've discovered our own spirituality. We draw on the great religious and philosophical traditions for wisdom, but as a package, no single one of them fulfills our need for truth, meaning and guidance. So we blend our knowledge of science, literature, and religious and philosophical traditions into an evolving, personalized faith.

When I was 15 and questioning my grandmother's religion, she responded with the prevailing cultural attitude: "If you don't believe it all, you might as well not bother." For centuries, believing it all has been the litmus test of whether you are a Christian or a heretic, one of "us" or one of "them." Your answer often had dramatic consequences, like finding your head tossed into a basket or mounted on a pole. The rejection is a little less overt today, but you can still smell it when people disparagingly refer to "my own spirituality" as the "mix and match" or "designer" religion trend.

Mix and match, designer, or my own spirituality, how could it be any other way? We are a different people than ever before, living in a world with challenges and choices never before experienced by other humans. More of us are more highly educated, socially and geographically mobile, and in daily contact with people from cultures other than our own. We're internally motivated, open to personal spiritual guidance, and aware that our path is our own, unique, but with common features. Not solo, but connected with and influencing the paths of others. We do not live in the world of our ancestors. And we know that their ways of understanding and living will not wholesale work for us.

Many of us are looking for something new. Not because of our superficiality or contemporary obsession with novelty and fads, but because the traditional isn't working and the novelties and fads are superficial, transient. We're looking for something that resonates deeply. Something real. We're looking for substance, truth, a universal core of spiritual knowledge and guidance that anchors us through continual change and allows us to live whole.

We are reaching a point in our collective evolution where a strong leader is no longer necessary, where we're recognizing our personal and collective influence and responsibility. We're no longer comfortable ignoring shades of gray, and we've outlived externally imposed morality and unexamined rules. Now we must rely on and refine our internal guidance and awareness. We are questioning and sloughing off inappropriate societal and cultural buts, shoulds and shouldn'ts, and opening ourselves to inner guidance, to our internal compass that is trained on universal principles. For that, we need our own spirituality.

NATURE'S POWER

A YEAR BEFORE I LEFT HOUSTON, a tropical storm dumped two days of unrelenting rain on our city. Hundreds of us walked, biked, or skated in the drenching downpour to lean over the bridges and watch Allen Parkway and Memorial Drive below turn into roiling rivers, submerging cars, vans, buses and delivery trucks under 30 feet of water. An evening newscaster was perplexed by why we were out in the storm. "It's dangerous," he fretted. "They should be home where it's safe."

Didn't he know? We were feeding our souls.

At first, I thought this was a Houstonian urge, so deprived are we of nature's moods. On the Texas Gulf Coast, there's little distinct seasonal variation, and the day-to-day changes are imperceptible unless you look closely. Mostly, it's sunny with shades of hot all year. Air-conditioning, in buildings and vehicles, is life. In the nearly 20 years I lived there, the natural world became a constant, steady drone, a taken-for-granted backdrop for human activity.

In Seattle, my post-Houston home, the sky, water and mountains change continually. They are palpably alive. From my window, downtown Seattle's 50-story buildings look like a Lego village, dwarfed by white-haired Mt. Rainier in the background 100 miles away. When that mammoth mountain erupts, it could wash us all into Puget Sound. Yet a native Seattleite complained, as we walked to a restaurant in just enough rain to bead on our jackets, "I don't like this drizzle. I like hard, pounding rain and thunder, the kind of storm that lets you know it's there. It rarely does that here."

This desire for natural extremes is widespread. In Arizona, a line of lightning rods and cabins attracts vacationers hoping to witness nature's electricity sizzling from pole to pole, even though they could get barbecued. Visitors from around the world brave 40 degree below zero weather to catch the aurora borealis streaming across the Alaskan sky. People hunker down with hurricane parties on the coasts, and camp out on Oregon's ocean beaches to watch Pacific storms roll in.

It's a soul thing, this thirst for nature's power displayed. Now that we humans have trashed the earth's skin, sucked the water, oil and minerals out of its veins, and insulated ourselves from its heat, cold, wind and rain, we seem to want evidence that our control over natural forces isn't absolute. That nature is still alive, still bigger and more powerful than we are, and still part of us.

Our culture has nearly eliminated the natural in human systems.

Separating the elderly and the young destroys our natural source of wisdom and of rejuvenation and growth. By living with our elders, we learn to accept the natural course of life. We see aging first-hand. We understand and expect that our bodies too will replace suppleness and firmness with wrinkles and sags, that our energy and our perspective on life will change with time and experience. By segregating the elderly from the young, we cut off our elders' natural means of revitalization, their immersion in the heart of life, and their place in the natural progression of generations. We stunt our own sense of history and belonging and leave the elderly lonesome, bored and waiting to die.

Nor do we have a natural way of dealing with our dead. With contemporary burial practices, we're embalmed and vaulted. The decomposing that naturally takes a decade or two could take a century or more. With cremation, decomposition takes only a few hours, so we're rushed away and may even believe that we have no right to lay our bodies in the earth when land is needed for the living.

The conscious awareness that we live on a living being that possesses the same life energy we do is growing. Some people are finding ways to live lightly on the earth. Many are trying to re-integrate the natural into existing systems, growing organic food, eating vegetarian, moving to rural areas, using wind and solar power, and struggling for limits via the WTO protests and biotechnology resistance.

But these attempts can get distorted when we try to do them within systems not conducive to them. For example, we move to the country and start trying to change it. We bring urban amenities, get rid of pests, ants, dust, and odors, and instead of becoming part of the existing community, we create a separate one, or keep to ourselves. We'll buy hormone-free meat, eco-fish, shade-grown coffee, and organic vegetables, if we can afford them, while the rest of our food system gets pumped full of hormones and synthetic substances.

Connected by spirit, we are not separate and cannot isolate ourselves. The wounds we create or leave for others will eventually return to us in one form or another through this connecting cord. Our systems need to change so these ways of living become the policy and practice of our society. When we create social systems that support and nourish the natural cycles, processes, and characteristics of life, they will support our physical, emotional and spiritual needs. If we don't, we'll make human life more vacuous, more vicious, and more toxic. We may ultimately destroy ourselves. But we won't destroy the planet. Mother Earth will shudder and shake us off, swallow us up, crush us under our own constructions. What naiveté or hubris to think otherwise! In the struggle for life, we're no match for the forces of the universe. We can learn to live in harmony with them, or they will live without us. Like all children, we are testing the limits.

THE POSITIVE SIDE OF VIOLENCE

IN THE DAYS AFTER THE SEPTEMBER 11 terrorist attacks, I wondered if I was the only person in the U.S. who retreated to lick my wounds and reflect. Every e-mail list I subscribe to, whether professional or personal interest, was thrown off-topic, taken over by furious, angry assertions of patriotism and revenge. Treasonous accusations were fired at anyone who urged restraint. Anyone who wanted to continue talking about the list topic was ignored or openly scorned.

I shut out the lists, turned off the television, and switched my car radio to tape. Friends and colleagues, some of whom needed the ongoing media accounts to help deal with their shock, filled me in on factual updates. I didn't want to experience the disaster over and over again, nor did I need to, to absorb its realness. Without watching the repeated pictures of disoriented survivors, frantic, weeping relatives, and smoke and fire, my heart split open. Stunned, I could think of little else, even in my dreams. I was hurt, sad and angry, and I needed to feel that—to feel all of the conflicting emotions of grief and let it work its way through me.

The saber-rattling and blustering, so banal and so futile, just added to my misery and sadness. Americans are an action-oriented bunch. We don't sit still long under normal circumstances, and when life is out of control, we're compelled to bring it quickly into line. However, on 9/11, except for the airlines, rescue workers and government officials, there was nothing for us to do. Adrenaline was pumping with nowhere to go. We were puffing up and making fierce noises like an animal trying to avert an attack. But there was no visible intruder kicking in our door. We were just throwing fire at each other to cover over the fact that we were all scared, confused and vulnerable.

Vulnerability is a fact of life American culture tries to control and ignore. We've been so successful at it that we've come to believe we're invulnerable. Life, we believe, should be risk-free. No one should ever be uncomfortable, feel pain or die unless they're bringing it on themselves by wrong thinking or wrong living. Or if they're elderly, in the case of dying. Even then, we believe the elderly should be able to control the way they die.

In this climate, violence is an illusion-buster. It penetrates our protective bubble and brings us face-to-face with our innate vulnerability. How we handle it determines the kind of society we create.

Vulnerability, faced openly rather than masked by fear, breeds humility. Accepting that we could need someone's help some day, that we might not always be able to pull our own weight, gives us empathy, compassion and generosity toward others. Pushing away that part of our humanity leaves us with anger, arrogance and bravado. The systems we develop reflect our choice: either recognizing and assisting us when we're vulnerable, or leaving us to fend for ourselves.

Living in the world conscious of our vulnerability requires trust and faith, in the universe, in other humans, in ourselves, in life. Separated from those qualities of the spirit, we've tried to replace them with control mechanisms and hide the damage when the mechanisms fail.

The damage violence causes spreads way beyond the victims, the families and the surrounding community. I realized the depth of its destruction while standing in line at a McDonald's restaurant in Houston. A few weeks earlier, a pick-up truck had rammed the plate glass windows of a Luby's restaurant in Fort Hood, Texas, 200 miles away. The driver jumped out firing an automatic rifle, terrorizing and killing captive diners. As I waited in line in Houston weeks later, a passing car backfired. Instantly, all dining room motion stopped. No one looked anywhere except at the door. Everyone stared, forgetting to breathe. When the car moved on, spitting from its tailpipe, we sipped our sodas in isolated silence.

Violence is so devastating that its effects lodge in our soul, yet we like to think the damage is swept away after the police tape is removed and clean-up crews leave. With no physical evidence of destruction, we are to believe that all has returned to normal.

But not everyone is willing to sustain this illusion. In the last couple of decades, murder sites have begun turning into impromptu shrines: flowers, flags, teddy bears, and notes piled on streets, sidewalks and fields where the killings happened. These spontaneous memorials attempt to repair the social and cultural damage violence creates. In the process, they refuse to allow either the damage or our vulnerability to be hidden. By injecting evidence of death into the daily lives of passersby, these shrines intrude on our ability to keep our own vulnerability at bay.

As horrendous as it is, violence can be a turning point—but it depends on how we deal with it. By integrating our innate vulnerability into conscious awareness, we can understand the deep roots and consequences of violence and commit to dealing honestly with them. Or we can stay on the surface, fearful and struggling to control the symptoms.

REDEFINING EXISTENCE

When my biracial nephew was born, twenty-one years ago, I thought, what a wonderful thing to be a person intimately familiar with more than one way of life. For some multiracial, multiethnic people, this may be the experience. But for many, it's just the opposite. Never feeling completely accepted in any world, living in a no-man's land between worlds. Or compelled to identify with one side or the other, tearing themselves apart. Simple, routine aspects of daily life most of us take for granted, like filling out forms for school, or work, or for personal needs such as a driver's license, are repeated reminders that they do not fit into the world's boxes.

But the boxes are falling apart. Boundaries are blurring. In addition to race and ethnicity, the traditional definition of family cannot hold when emotional, psychological, financial and child-rearing ties are between ex-spouses, cohabitating couples and same sex partners.

As more of us leave hometowns to relocate across countries and continents, communities and support networks are no longer simply the people with whom we were raised or those living in our neighborhood. When bikers work as massage therapists and bankers sport tattoos, occupation carries less identifying weight.

The medical system creates boundary crossings and quandaries galore. Test-tube babies grown-up and questioning their parentage, organ transplant recipients wondering about the donors whose heart beats inside them. Even birth and death, which used to be fairly simply defined, now swirl in debates about when life begins and ends.

Such ambiguity is inherent in redefining existence. And that's what we've been doing for the last half of the Twentieth Century. When the U.S. dropped the atomic bombs that ended World War II, the awesome power of technology to destroy life planted itself in our global consciousness. A dozen years later, the first successful human organ transplants showed the equally awesome power of technology to sustain life. Then we landed on the moon. In only a few decades, the boundaries of human existence expanded inward and outward.

With the power to take, give and alter all life, in an instant, and globally communicate that change in a matter of minutes, we have created a world like no other in human history. Our ability to create and manipulate technology gives us tremendous control over our physical world. But such power is precarious, full of promise, dread and contradictions.

Life is growing ever more complex. We have decisions to make that no humans have ever had to face. Yet our fundamental approach to dealing with life has changed little. We still try to separate it into groups we can identify or identify with, or parts we can comprehend and apply predetermined solutions to. We still want to reduce life to a pill or an equation, or put it in a box where we know how to think and act toward it and how it will behave.

This dualistic, categorical perspective contradicts our multifaceted, multidimensional nature. We are not just our gender, our profession, or our familial roles. Nor are we solely physical creatures. Yet American society focuses its progress and power primarily on physical development, ignoring and undervaluing the social, psychological, cultural and spiritual aspects of life rather than giving equal weight to their expansion.

This lopsided emphasis has thrown life out of balance, separated us from each other and all that we are. When life is not allowed to be whole, the damage erupts in all the ways we see and in ways we don't yet recognize. But it can also prompt us to question who we really are, and the relevance of our cultural beliefs. We can begin to go our own way, to transcend the existing system or established norms, to live outside them and even change them.

Many people are dealing with the false dichotomies and arbitrary lines of race by simply refusing to specify a racial identity, or by checking all the boxes. After years of pressure from interracial groups, the U.S. Census Bureau finally altered its 2000 census form to allow responses in multiple race categories. But our systems—

government, industry, and education—are too bulky, entrenched and slow to change culture. They are purveyors of culture.

To come to grips with the complexity of human nature and the world that nature has created, we will need to learn to live whole, using guideposts and identifiers in addition to the physical. With expanded consciousness and capabilities that allow us to see commonality, work across boundaries, and where appropriate, dissolve them, individuals, not institutions, will have to lead the way.

THE CENOTAPH MIRROR

WANDERING IN A NINETEENTH century cemetery, I noticed a tall stone marker. In addition to a long list of community organizations this man participated in, the epitaph said that he died when his ship, the *Rights of Man*, sank in the New Orleans harbor. I scoffed and snorted. Yeah right, what kind of advertising slogan is this?! *The Rights of Man*, puh! I didn't buy its sincerity for a moment.

As I continued my tombstone scouting, my irritation subsided and a mild discomfort, like sitting on the crack between chairs rather than squarely in the seat, started tugging at me. Why had I responded so automatically and so vehemently to this cenotaph? There was a message there. Something I needed to understand about it. The answer didn't come quickly. This one needed to gestate. It needed time to make itself clear to me. And when it did, months later, it wasn't about the epitaph or the name of the vessel at all. Those were just triggers. The message was about me, and about our culture.

Against my nature, I had become cynical. But I couldn't see it without this cenotaph mirror reflecting it back to me. *Hey, I'm not cynical, just realistic. This is the way the world is. Everybody's hustling for a buck and they use anything they can. Play on babies and motherhood and apple pie, and religion and even the founding documents of U.S. American democracy. It's all to promote something about themselves. It don't mean nothin'!* Whew! When I saw that I'd moved so far away from who I really am, that I'd somehow lost connection to the great expanse, I cried. My body shuddered and the wall I'd built crumbled. The light poured in. Suddenly the universe of possibility and mystery opened up again.

Then I realized, this cynical attitude was not only true for me, it's true of our contemporary world. We look back from our position in the 21st Century and believe no one could possibly be serious about such noble ideals. We see only the limits of their vision and how far short of the goal they fell. If we make an idealistic statement today, we apologize for it in the same breath. We know it's kind of fluffy and mushy, kind of unrealistic. No one today would name their ship after an ideal, a constant reminder of an existence greater than our own immediate surroundings, an existence that's worth striving for. Today, we name our boats "Pleasure Cruise" and "Sextasy" and "Indulgence," or we give them company names.

In this kind of culture, we have to shovel a lot to unearth that spark within us, to open an oxygen path so it can ignite. Yet we yearn for ignition. We long to live in a world of substance and truth, where exerting ourselves is worth the effort. It's this desire with no place to go that creates cynicism, an equal and opposite reaction to idealism.

But where was I to go, now that I'd re-opened to possibility? How could I keep this released energy alive? As soon as I asked these questions, I heard the answers intuitively. What was I doing to create the world I wanted to live in? Not much. I was committed to trying to live my own life according to the values I espouse, but I wasn't engaged in the world at large, and I needed to be. That engagement needed to be a balanced engagement, unlike my ten-year absorption in social work that deep-fried me and made me retreat to computers and data. I needed to retain my idealism, to hold onto my vision of the world, but temper it with patience and wisdom. Inner flames need to burn evenly and continuously, instead of blazing and destroying the house.

I wonder, as a nation, what is our vision? What is our guiding direction or the 21st Century ideal we'd paint on the side of our ship? Do we have one? Or do we simply react to quarterly reports and the current crisis? There is no shortage of worthwhile issues—new, complicated, diffuse issues that are difficult to grasp, like the global economy and population control. Some are species and environment altering, like genetic engineering, toxic waste, climate change, and AIDS. Then there are our recalcitrant issues that just keep finding new forms, like racial profiling, cultural intrusion, and teen homicide and terrorism.

It's easy to feel inconsequential in the face of such complex, global issues. How do we have an impact? Where can we grab hold? My inclination is to retreat and hope I can find a safe spot out of the fray. Yet everything we do, including trying to hide, has an effect. Living between death and birth, as we are, in the tumultuous currents of the old world dying and the new one being born, we are shaping this new world. The question is whether we're doing it unconsciously—or intelligently in full awareness of our vision.

All That We Are

Experience is spirit's way of showing us who we are and what we're capable of. At times, this experiencing is intentional. A career promotion or a voluntary move to a new culture can expand our awareness and draw out traits we never knew we possessed. At other times, circumstances are thrust upon us, such as illness, job loss, divorce, or a loved one's death.

Any experience that moves us out of our comfort zone can be an opening to our spirit—if we allow it. If we're willing to take the risk, to look silly, to ask difficult questions of ourselves and of the world and to hear the answers, even if we don't like what we hear....if we allow ourselves to be uncomfortable, to stand on shaky ground, to tolerate the insecurity and uncertainty, the lack of control...if we immerse ourselves in the experience, flow with it, and allow our spirit's insights to emerge and become part of who we are.

When I was growing up, regardless of my career choice or life plan of the day, my refrain for adult life was, "I don't want to be bored." At the time, I'd never heard the adage, "Be careful what you ask for, you just might get it." Nor did I realize then how literal the universe can be, or the surprising ways that wishes can be fulfilled.

My life has been a series of ongoing changes, difficult choices, and non-obvious pleasures. I've lived on a farm, in small towns, and in major cities. Money—I've had plenty, none, and amounts in between. I've lived in a house stuffed full of people, lived alone, and lived and worked with people of different races, cultural backgrounds, social status, and lifestyles. I've worked dayshifts and nightshifts, in restaurants, nursing homes, a mental institution and clinic, in education, and journalism, and I've researched, experienced, and now speak about death and dying. Through all of it, my spirit is alive and teaching me.

So as I resisted writing *Natural Urges*, I was surprised when my spirit's message to me was "Have the courage to travel the road where your talent takes you—even into the dark places." *I've traveled the dark places as much as I care to,* I argued. *I deserve a rest.* In the last few years I've developed a challenging, enjoyable, professional career with a good income. I'm fortunate to be in a loving and supportive intimate relationship. We live in a comfortable home, travel often, and spend our leisure time as we please. I am content.

But spirit longs to live whole. Expression, expansion, and experience are its nourishment. As I've learned to live by the world's rules, I've curtailed my voice, locked it away, dulled it, hammered it into submission, dropped it below a whisper until it became so inaudible I believed I didn't even have one. But as a writer, my voice is an essential part of who I am. My spirit, my inner voice, will not allow an amputation. To be all that I am, my inner voice must be my outer voice.

When we are in touch with spirit, living from our core, we are secure regardless of external circumstances or emotional upheaval. Extreme conditions can temporarily warp personalities. We can lose worldly identities. But our spirit's oneness with the universe, our essence, is an internal refuge, our source of support and guidance when the dark places threaten to overwhelm. In opening to, trusting, and flowing with our spirit, we discover all that we are.

SHIFTING GEARS

When I was born, my mother and I both nearly died. She labored three days to push me out while I pushed back, trying to go the opposite direction. At least that's the way my mother tells it. "It's impossible for a baby to push back," a friend told me. Another friend says my birth story is a psychological set-up, a way that my family's conflicts were transferred to and focused on me.

Whatever the physiological facts of labor, or the conflictual family dynamics, for me the essential truth of my birth is that I tried to change my mind at the last minute. I was born to fulfill a life of growth and service, but when the time came to slide out of my warm cocoon into the bright light and noise of the physical world, I balked. The close-up realization that I would for a lifetime be constrained by the limits of my physical body and the earth plane, doused my commitment. The path I knew I'd travel, with its obstacles, deprivations, and grueling lessons—that suddenly seemed to far outweigh its gifts and pleasures—was enough to make me try to back out of the deal.

I'm not certain my birth experience is a memory I retained from before or at the moment my spirit entered this body. As my friends point out, so many other potential explanations exist, including metaphor or fantasy. Perhaps my perspective on my birth is a childhood interpretation based on experiences, like remembering my mother's version of the story as I began to realize the disjuncture between my nature and the workings of this world. But while writing this essay, as I again questioned the source of my birth story, a scene in the documentary *Amargosa* covered me with confirmation chills.

The film is about Marta Beckett, a dancer and artist who performed in New York in the 1940s and 50s and still does in a renovated opera house in Death Valley, Nevada. At one point, Beckett relates her experience of her own birth.

"I was in the corner of the room, near the ceiling," she said. "I could see my mother, my father and the nurse. A breeze was blowing through the room and the nurse told my father to shut the window." Finally, I felt, here is a real, living person who recalls her birth as a conscious experience.

Most of us believe people can't remember their own birth. An infant brain is not developed enough to store memories. But what if memories are stored elsewhere, in a non-physical, non-chemical medium? In the spirit? With an infant's inability to speak, and our adult disconnection from our own spirit, how would we know what depth of awareness newborns experience or bring with them into the world?

When I was thirty, through the hospital nursery window, I saw my youngest niece for the first time and sensed her magnanimous spirit. I could see grandness surfacing again when, before she could talk, her frustration with her body's inability to communicate spilled out. The tension in her neck, her pursed lips, puffed cheeks, and clenched fists; she was bursting with conversation yet couldn't get the flesh apparatus that contained her to work. William, an e-mail acquaintance, remembers when he was a child learning to speak. He'd wondered why he should babble when E.S.P. was so easy and readily available.

Language is a tool of the physical world and physical bodies. My direct spiritual experiences as an adult often involve neither thought nor language, until I try to interpret or communicate the experiences. The experience and its meaning or insight is whole and self-evident. Words can't express it without taking it apart.

In writing this book, I struggle to convey feelings, impressions, subtle awareness, insights, and experiences, with words, some of which are not even good approximations of the realities of spirit. And I struggle to shape paragraphs and pages into a structure that barely mimics the flow of the spiritual process. I'm attempting too, as much as possible, to avoid language that carries such heavy cultural baggage that the words themselves obscure experience, halt thinking, and divide us into warring camps.

Language has its limitations. Yet it's the primary mechanism we use to try to understand each other and make sense of our world. Cultures generally possess many words for well-known and important experiences and phenomena, few words for the unknown or unaccepted. The more we recognize and accept spirit's language, the richer the word language we'll develop to communicate the experiences. Conversely perhaps, the more we understand, accept, and learn to use spirit's communicative abilities, the less we'll need spoken or written language to explain.

Although language is a major material world characteristic we adapt to, it's not the only one. Before he could walk, William, the E.S.P. child, remembers his mother calling him from across the room. Immediately he moved to her, yet she continued calling his name. This experience happened a few times before he realized his body wasn't traveling with him. It remained sitting on the floor, unable to stand.

A friend told me about a childhood disappointment. When Sue was four years old, she saw a pair of glittery red shoes in her dream. She was thrilled to get them and fully expected to see the shoes beside her toy box when she woke up. When the shoes failed to materialize, she realized that in *this* world, things won't appear just by thinking that they will.

My friends Andre and Marian believe in reincarnation and permit their children's other-realm expressions. Yet they were surprised when their three-year-old son met Andre's colleague, Doug, for the first time and addressed him as Juan Pedro. Doug too was surprised.

He was aware of a past life in which he was a soldier named Juan Pedro, but he never considered that others might recognize him by that name in this life.

Perhaps this segmentation and separation, this amnesia vis-à-vis our spirit's home and natural abilities have been necessary: to keep us here and allow us to learn and adapt to the necessities of living in the material world with minimal confusion. As consciousness expands, however, and the unseen and material worlds draw closer, we'll know from experience the continuity and overlap between beings and realms. We'll be able to navigate these multiple layers and dimensions with ease. And we'll understand that the talents, abilities, and knowing we bring into this life have application in the physical world.

BEYOND THE SKIN

A SKILL I'VE FOUND HELPFUL is my ability to immediately extract the essence of a person, some central characteristic that eventually shows itself in their behavior. Often I know on sight, even before talking with them, if they're trustworthy, or selfish, or controlling, or some quality that's important for me to be aware of. People carry this energy with them. They can't rid themselves of it. Because it's part of them, not a transient state, this energy is concentrated and accessible to others who can sense it. This sensing is a valuable survival skill—likely the reason why those of us who know we possess it, developed it. Not all is bliss in either the physical world or the universe. We need to survive and protect others. The more tools we possess, the better our chances.

Like most of my intuitive abilities, this sensing doesn't kick in with everyone I meet. And it's spontaneous, not something I think through or consciously attempt to do. For that reason, I hold the information lightly. Meaning that it's registered in my consciousness, but I try not to solidify it there and let it become a lens through which I view all of the person's actions. Because people are multi-faceted, they don't always act from a single motivation or a cohesive core, especially if they're not well integrated. But when they do behave in a way that's consistent with what I perceived about them from the start, the consistency cues up my recollection of my initial impression. Given my penchant for doubting, I inwardly smile at the validation.

Temporal, transient states also carry energy that some people can perceive. In the last few years, I've experienced a few spontaneous, visual recognitions of this energy. The first was at a friend's father's funeral. As I listened to the speakers leading the service and eulogizing him, I realized I was watching colors shimmer around each speaker's head and shoulders. The colors differed, blue, purple, silver, orange, green, yellow, with each person, as did the colors' intensity, the height of the energy field, and the rate and pattern of its movement. In addition to this energy, a faded, blotchy white shadow stood slightly behind and beside the main speaker.

Surprised at seeing this, I initially just cued into the fact that I was watching. But then I started wondering if I was really seeing what I was seeing, wondering what it was, and why it was happening then and there. Doubt made it vanish. As I tried to bring it back, I turned sideways and could again see the colors in my peripheral vision. But it was a strain. So I focused again on the speaker's words, relaxed and put the colors out of my mind. Eventually they appeared again. I could see them straight on. This time I just watched, and listened, without questioning. That still didn't erase my doubts though, or my desire for confirmation. So when we left the funeral, I asked my partner if she saw anything other than the speakers. After a strange look and a "no," I told her what I saw and openly questioned what and why. I now know that this visual recognition is similar to the non-visual, intuitive sensing I've always possessed, but it provides more than a single point of information.

Our spirit doesn't lie. We learn to control our language, and even our body language, to present the image we choose, but the spirit can't be manipulated or hidden from those who can see. As our species evolves, perceiving beyond the physical is an ability we'll develop to help us deal with the complexities of our world. At this point in time, our technology has pushed beyond what our physicality is capable of understanding and so creates quandaries we have no way to handle.

Like racial profiling. Observing skin color is a crude, inefficient method of determining risk that sparks so many moral dilemmas we can't sort them all out and decide what to do. To balance protection and justice, we must move to a higher level of discernment. We must learn to tap into and understand these subtler forms of identifying character and intent.

POWERFUL THOUGHTS

When I worked in a mental health clinic, occasionally a patient made me wonder how we draw the lines between mental illness and spiritual experiences and abilities.

Planes swooping out of the air vents dropping bombs. Knife-wielding devils chasing clinic staff to cut out their hearts. These were run of the mill psychoses that I never seriously questioned. With such disturbing thoughts and images whirling in their heads, these people couldn't function. They couldn't hold a job, couldn't live alone, couldn't make friends, and some couldn't even handle minimal hygiene needs. Their illnesses were incapacitating.

But then I encountered Randy who swore his thoughts maimed other people, for which he suffered excruciating guilt. Once, mad at his friend Paul, Randy wished Paul would burn his hand on the stove. He did. Usually though, Randy didn't will destruction on people.

The thoughts just entered his mind, randomly. He might think of a car accident, a fall down a flight of stairs, or a broken arm for a family member, acquaintance or public figure. Soon after, he learned the outcome. A phone call, a knock on the door, or a news report. Then his guilt fired up.

In my office, tipped forward in his chair, Randy would plead with me to believe him and help make these destructive thoughts stop. His sincerity, and the similarity between his experiences and my own precognitive knowing made me queasy and drew prickly shivers along my spine. Randy was mentally ill. How could I believe his thoughts influenced others? And yet, many people would not believe my spiritual experiences, even though I knew them to be real. So I had to consider the possibility of truth in Randy's experience.

Thoughts *do* have power. Our thinking can change the way we feel, the way we act, and subsequently the course of events. If I think my colleague's insensitive remark was an attempt to undermine me and elevate his status in the eyes of our boss, I get angry. I can decide to confront him, or snub him, or get back at him, or let the resentment fester and seep out in snide remarks. If I think that same insensitive remark was said because my colleague lacked all the information, or just wasn't thinking carefully about his speech, I may be hurt, or disappointed, or I may feel no pain at all. I then decide to provide him with the missing data, or talk with him about how his remark affected me, or just let it go. Any of these thought-action patterns can create a different chain of events.

Thoughts possess power, and speech even more so. Words said in haste, without anger or another strong emotion attached, carry diffuse energy that moves neither forcefully nor far. We say the words, others hear them, and we all forget them. This is the energy level of most of our daily conversation.

Repeated phrases we say to others, or to ourselves, soak into the unconscious where the energy accumulates. Eventually this energy may solidify as a physical characteristic or event. We know that telling a child he's stupid may produce an adult who lacks confidence and cannot learn. If I tell myself that the world is unfair, and I repeat the refrain whenever life doesn't conform to my expectations, eventually I may become bitter, give up trying, and find myself experiencing even more injustice. Conversely, if my internal dialogue repeatedly tells me I can never fail, I may achieve enormous success.

But can our thoughts *directly* influence the behavior of others? Animals, sensing that they're being watched, either flee or turn to watch the watcher. People do this too. A friend who teaches in elementary school told me that when her class gets rowdy, she holds calmness in her mind. Often, the children settle down without her telling them to.

So could Randy be wreaking havoc on people using mental powers? He couldn't work, couldn't drive a car, rarely left his house, chain-smoked, and shook so violently he always wore his coffee. How could this man's thoughts possess that kind of power?

On the few occasions when I've tried to project thought energy outward, it's required concentration. Like my elementary teacher friend, I had to hold the thought still. Randy was always so visibly anxious, I doubted he could focus on a single thought long enough or intently enough to make it manifest physically. Perhaps Randy was attributing cause and effect where there was none. Maybe he was picking up events precognitively, but not causing those events. Randy didn't buy that possibility. He wanted me to believe him. I wanted to understand how his experience differed from mine.

In American culture, when a person is labeled mentally ill, attempts by others to understand stop, and efforts to control and eliminate the behavior begin. A person whose mind can't be trusted to reason and perceive appropriately within a prescribed range is often feared or discounted. On our way into a museum, Susan, one of the six patients on our outing, pointed to a bronze covered hole in the sidewalk and wondered aloud what it was. "Maybe it's a door to another world," I joked.

"Hmmm," she sneered. "If I said that, they'd increase my medication."

Again those spiky chills crawled across my skin. Being misunderstood is one of the reasons I've been reluctant to voice my spiritual experiences and knowledge. If people knew about my experiences, then heard me say what I said in jest, it would color their interpretation. They may not take me seriously anymore. They would doubt my ability to reason. And science, my primary method for understanding the world, relies on reason, clear thinking, logic, rigor...and reputation.

The scientific method creates problems in the social sciences, where factors can't be neatly compartmentalized and distinguished. Nor can the effects of a single characteristic be isolated and used to fully explain an event, trend or behavior such as mental illness. In building a model for researching aging in one of my sociology courses, the professor asked the class for variables to include. My classmates suggested age, race, gender, living arrangements, and health. I suggested spirituality. His quizzical look betrayed his quandary: how could a bright student give such an idiotic answer? Apparently he decided I was joking and asked for "serious" responses.

At another point in my quest for a degree, I wanted to study the sociology of the paranormal, not whether these experiences exist or are real, but how we respond to the reported experiences, how cultures dismiss or incorporate these claims, and the effects of extrasensory experiences on the experiencers. No such field existed. It took weeks for the department staff to find a professor willing to oversee my study and she tentatively agreed, pursuant to meeting me and, I suppose, determining whether my ideas were interesting and sensible or if I was a flake.

There's no place in science for spirit or soul, except in the scientists themselves of course. Our scientific method can't address spirit. It won't fit into the box. Apparently, even studying consciousness phenomena is looked on askance. I was surprised to find a website (www.issc-taste.org/index.shtml) that offers a comfort zone specifically for scientists to share their extrasensory experiences with other scientists.

Oddly, graduate school not only led to my spiritual nature

flying free, it showed me the limitations of the scientific paradigm in understanding and explaining human experience, the rigidity of the academic culture's mindset, and the duels over ideology that are so like religious wars.

Applied science is wonderful for manipulating the physical world, but life is far too big to be confined to a single method of understanding and living. For example, we can exchange organs with each other, but how do we ask and make that decision when a loved one suddenly dies? What are our obligations and who do we become if we accept a piece of another's body? How do we understand that another died, while we live on? We can artificially inseminate, but what about the artificially-produced progeny when they question their parentage and genetics? We can keep alive single-pound premature infants in neonatal hospital units. But what about the family's roller coaster ride as the newborn's prognosis shifts from hour to hour? We can build suicide machines. But who stays and who goes? And who decides?

These are spiritual issues, dilemmas of contemporary human existence that can't be fully grasped through the reasoning mind. Until we learn to access and work on deeper levels, we'll continue to rely on the magnificence and limitations of high-technology and struggle with the *dis-ease* it produces. Eventually we may be able to regenerate our own organs, instead of borrowing another's. We may learn to dress the wounds that lodge in our spirit, and come to understand the nature of new beginnings. Maybe we'll even accept death, when it's time to die.

ENERGY EXCHANGES

We know that body language reveals more than our words convey. Yet we relate to and communicate with each other on even subtler levels, usually unconsciously.

Last year, I attended a meeting organized by a man I knew by reputation as demanding, abrasive and quick to hurl groundless complaints that he vehemently and viciously defends. Having never met Ben myself, I didn't want his reputation to color my attitude and behavior toward him, so I spent a few minutes beforehand breathing deeply, clearing my mind, and opening myself, preparing to perceive and act on only the information and dynamics of the meeting.

The five of us sat around the table talking for about twenty minutes, when suddenly I felt like I was being pushed out of my body. No fear, just this strange dissociated feeling. Like I was slightly above, behind and to the right of my physical self. At the same time I felt a tangible, yet invisible presence between this man and me. That presence was doing the pushing.

Responding to this out-of-kilter state, I simply settled back into my body. My return was smooth, easy and automatic. I felt centered, solid, secure, and curious about what had happened. My first thought was that this guy's energy was not centered, not contained within him, nor was it controlled. I'm still not sure exactly what this experience was. The conversation between Ben and me was neither intimidating nor hostile, yet at another level we were interacting, perhaps carrying on the struggle both of us had decided not to do in the physical.

Learning to distinguish our own energies from the energies of others, without separating ourselves from people, is a challenge of the physical world. Spiritual energy is the cord that connects us to each other and all life. Yet, to manifest in the physical, this energy must filter through our body, personality, cultural beliefs and values, and even the residue of our experiences. Like lenses, these filtering mechanisms break the energy, refracting it the way crystal separates light into multiple and distinct colors. When we unknowingly act from one or more bands of the spectrum, rather than the whole, or refuse to accept the type of energy these bands contain, we can get snared or derailed by others' energy, give our own energy away, or allow others to usurp it.

This energy diffusion, or *dis-integration*, shows itself in an infinite variety of behaviors. In the late 1980's, when Multiple Personality

Disorder was the hot new psychiatric label, one of the clients on my caseload carried the diagnosis, mistakenly I believed. She was hospitalized repeatedly for her violent behavior. She would cut up her husband's clothes, smash all the dishes, set fire to the living room carpet, or attack him.

She possessed two personalities, she told me, the "good June" and the "bad June." The "bad June" of course was the personality that landed her in the psych ward. After every hospital release, her husband established more drastic restrictions. At first he locked her in a single room when he left for work. Eventually, he began tying her to the bed, then would return home every few hours to check on her. So convinced was she of her diagnosis, my suggesting that perhaps she had reason to be angry brought on a berating of the "bad June" and a litany of her offenses. Maintaining the split allowed June to distance herself from her unacceptable behavior and avoid dealing with a failing marriage, but at the price of perverting and abandoning her own power.

Anger is a common dis-integrated energy in American society, especially among women. People who project a honey-and-roses demeanor also subtly exude a seething underside that some can more deeply submerge than others. They fear anger, their own and that of others, and so they cannot soothe and integrate their rage into their concept of who they are. Anger is a powerful energy, most visible in its destructive form. But this same energy manifests in determination and strength. If we avoid or deny this force out of fear of its potential effects, we do indeed become ineffective.

A body's sickness, an entrenched personality trait, or a traumatic experience can sometimes become a barrier that completely blocks one's spiritual energy. These people, unable to participate in the world's constant energy flow, can extract the energy of others, without either person being consciously aware of the exchange.

Ann invited a friend to stay at her house while both of them were experiencing hard times. Anticipating they would support each other, Ann found instead that her friend was stealing so she asked the woman to leave. A few mornings later, while Ann lay in bed in that half-asleep, half-awake state, her friend walked into the bedroom, softly said goodbye and touched Ann's foot. Though still asleep, Ann felt energy whoosh out of her body. Suddenly, strange occurrences that had puzzled her all made sense; the crow rasping outside the window every morning until the friend left for the day, periodically hearing the refrain from a Bob Marley song, "Your best friend could be your worst enemy," and how drained and confused Ann felt with her friend at times.

Energy exchanges go on all the time, and not all exchanges are detrimental. People can willingly blend their energies, to achieve a common goal, in healing rites, or in making love. We experience energy interactions in physical and emotional behavior. If we could see the actual energy transference, it would look like what it feels like; pulling, pushing, bending, colliding, grating, sucking, blending, or bolstering.

The more integrated and centered we become, the easier it is to identify others' energy and to share our energy and replenish it. Integrated energy is concentrated energy. Like water springing from the earth rather than trickling in a river's tributary, integrated energy is closer to the source, to pure spirit. Its power is present and available. Some people can intentionally focus certain bands of the spectrum for a specific purpose such as healing, calming, stimulating, or protecting. With a direct tap to the source, their energy replenishes automatically. As long as they rest when tired, eat when hungry, and care for their physical and psychological needs, they can readily share their energy without diminishing their own supply.

CAN WE CHOOSE?

IN THE LATE 1970's, the State of Missouri closed down its worst St. Louis nursing homes and moved some of the most debilitated residents to the facility I worked in, 100 miles away. Mr. Williams was in a coma. His sturdy, 50-year-old athletic body was rigid, frozen in time except for the bedsores that ate away the brown, pink and yellow-white layers of flesh on his heels, hips, elbows and shoulder blades.

Every day I bathed and lotioned this man, cleaned and bandaged his wounds, repositioned his body to take the pressure off, and talked and sang to him. "You never know with a coma, whether someone will wake up," we were told. "Talking to him just might help."

I'd been washing, bandaging, talking and singing in Mr. William's room for months when, leaning over his bed, a bass voice in front of me asked, "What time is it?"

Huh? I stared at him, uncertain. Then his eyes, as immobile as the rest of his body, moved. "Three fifty-two" I said, focusing on the clock as if it were a magic stone, a link between this world and the next, or maybe it had issued a wake up call.

In the long silence that followed—which was only a matter of seconds, but time stretches when the unimaginable happens—I couldn't quite believe I'd heard him. Then he said, "Thank you." I turned the clock so he could see it on his own.

When I think back on it now, I wonder why I never asked him where he was all those months. Was his consciousness trapped in that inflexible body, flat and deflated? Was he out flying around somewhere listening, just waiting for the right time to return to the physical? Or was he trying to make up his mind, to return or leave forever?

Does everyone have a choice to live or die? I know I did. About the same time I was caring for Mr. Williams, I had to make the decision for myself.

Driving along a rural highway flanked by harvested fall cornfields, the flat Missouri delta stretched to the horizon, as endless as the stream of pain and confusion in my life. Whatever the catastrophe was that day, it was one too many. I'd reached my limit. If the first eighteen years were the measure for the next eighteen or thirty or fifty, I wanted out.

In the distance, the road swelled and bent into an "S" to cross over a railroad track. This was my opportunity. An easy exit. I pressed the accelerator and raced toward the curves intending to shoot past the guardrail. The Chevelle climbed the sharp rise and the right front tire dropped off the pavement with a thunk. Suddenly, the steering wheel spun free. A tie rod broke. The car was out of my control and I panicked, clinging to the useless circle.

Immediately I heard, not with my ears but with my mind, "You can go if you want, but if you stay, you must promise never to try this again." Deliberation time was zero. Without words, or thought, I chose. The car swung back onto the pavement, skidded around the curves and stopped off the shoulder of the road at the base of the hill as if I'd intentionally parked it just a bit too close to the ditch.

I don't know who I made a promise to. Even so, I'm not one to go back on my word. For years I questioned and raged at the voice. What was it? How could I have the choice to live or die, or the power to gain control of that broken vehicle? If not me, then what force took control? And why *should* I keep my vow when it was made during such distress and peril that I really had no choice? Clearly, I did have a choice, but a decade passed before I accepted that my decision was freely made.

My friend Gail knows with equal certainty that, while stricken with a serious illness, she had no option to live or die. Unconscious and running a high fever for three days, Gail "heard" voices debating whether she should return. "The cord is terribly frayed," she recalls someone saying. When Gail regained consciousness, she was angry. Strangers had made the decision without giving her a choice or even asking her preference. She insists the voices were not doctors and is convinced that this decision-making occurred in a non-physical realm she could hear, but not see.

How much choice do we have, and in what aspects of our life? From my earliest childhood memories, I sensed I was born for a specific purpose. I didn't know the details, but I knew I had work to do—tasks and responsibilities in addition to the usual fare of life. By the time I attempted suicide, I no longer believed it or cared. If a job needs to be done, let somebody else do it, I thought, in the rare instances I thought about my purpose at all.

Perhaps we're all on earth for a specific purpose, or a call. I know we're all here to learn and grow. We carry with us energies that manifest as relationships, personality, talents, issues, and lessons. Our lessons can be learned in many ways, just as purpose can be carried out in many ways. The details are not scripted or pre-set, but are the result of a web of simultaneous events and circumstances.

In my mid-twenties, I was deeply involved with a spiritual group. Over time, the group dynamics changed, becoming tighter, more constraining and controlling. Loyalty tests began. And if our spiritual progress was adequate, we were supposed to have refined our intuition so keenly that we no longer needed to ask questions or discuss any actions the group leaders might take. We were all supposed to intuitively know we were on the right course.

I've never taken anything at face value. So I refused to relinquish my need to question, and life in the group got tense. I knew leaving

Natural Urges

was the only option, but the decision was grueling. My purpose in life is a spiritual one. What if, like the group members said, I was just being stubborn. What if, by leaving, I was turning my back on what I was born to do—denying my destiny.

I couldn't eat, sleep or work for days. I begged for answers, but all that came was my spirit's nudging me away from the group. So right or wrong, I endured their wrath and my own suffering and walked away. The best consolation I could come up with at the time was, if a spiritual calling is my purpose, the opportunity will come around again. It took years for that explanation to ease my worry. Then I learned it wasn't the whole truth.

We *can* miss our destiny. I was responding intensely to my calling, but the circumstances weren't right. The group was going wrong. I wasn't strong enough to allow my first spirituality book to be published. And I had too many other obstacles to overcome.

When we have a purpose to fulfill, our spirit will keep pushing until there's no hope—until we draw our last breath and this life is done. But, to some degree at least, we have free will. Sometimes the environmental circumstances will never be right. We may never feel strong enough, or wise enough, or prepared enough. Still, it's up to us to answer our calling, our purpose—or forego the call.

HIDDEN TALENTS

IN A RECENT DISCUSSION ABOUT SPIRIT ENERGY, an e-mail acquaintance told me to hold my hands, palms facing each other, against a solid background. "Move them slightly," she said, "and you'll see energy." So I experimented.

I wasn't expecting to see anything, but I wasn't doubting either. Like a blank page, I was accepting of whatever occurred, even if nothing happened. Facing a white wall, my hands about four inches apart, I felt heat between them. Within a minute or two, I saw yellow on the wall, the width of the distance between my hands. But nothing between my hands except the warmth. *I'll try it again sometime and see if anything different happens*, I thought.

I hit the send button to relay my experience, then shut down the computer. Lighting incense and a white candle, I drew a bubble bath. In the warm, frothy water, I relaxed again into an open state of acceptance, raised my hands together and slowly tilted them, one toward me and one away, like a vertical seesaw. Smoky white streams curled off my palms and fingertips. Transparent blue flickers turned into undulating ribbons, weaving themselves into the white plumes. I watched, in recognition but without thought, until a swirling, blue-silver ball about the size of an apple appeared, sitting between my hands without touching my skin. Seeing the ball awed me, though, and I reverted to my habitual response. I questioned, skeptically, and dropped my hands into the water. The ball, of course, disappeared.

Because doubt is my spirit killer, I had committed myself to acceptance and curious, rather than judgmental, questioning. So my untrusting reaction annoyed me. I wanted to make it right. I put my hands together again, but the energy didn't show immediately. When it did, I saw a thin silver-white and green tint along the palm-side of my fingertips. No streaming. This energy appeared nearly solid, its movement barely perceptible. I associate green with healing, and I had a swollen gland, so I touched my right hand to the sore lump and focused my thought on wellness. Later, I repeated this hands-on while I lay in bed falling asleep.

In the morning, as I readied myself for work, the sore spot drained. That evening, most of the soreness and all of the swelling was gone.

Healing is not high on my agenda. I'm healthy, and no longer work in a human service field, so I don't think about or experience illness often. But this self-healing reminded me of a similar experience and made me wonder if healing, in some form, is part of my life purpose.

Twenty years ago, in my mid-twenties, I fractured my ankle. Returning from the doctor's office, I pressed my hand to the break, directed green thought energy to it, then wrapped green cloth around my foot and lower leg. After three days, I walked normally, without pain, and without crutches. My follow-up appointment, six weeks later, was a needless visit.

The night after my gland swelling disappeared, falling asleep was, uncharacteristically, a long process. From midnight to 1:30 a.m., I rolled and squirmed and hugged my pillow before finally going to lie on the couch. Within minutes, I saw a fleeting image of myself (in my mind, not with my eyes) leaning into and holding onto the side of a massive rock cliff at the ocean's edge. In this vision, my right arm, stretching along the stone, pointed across the water toward the setting sun. A laser-thin green light, arched and miles-long, flowed from the tip of my index finger and vanished like the rainbow's end, in the waves.

After these energy experiences and this vision, I now know I am, at least sometimes, capable of transmitting healing energy. But I'm not sure my role is physically healing people. My partner, Jul, recently developed back pain and began physical therapy, so we decided to try a test. As I massaged her, I could see a long dark strip running along one side of her back from mid-ribcage to hip, and with the palm of my left hand, I felt a hot spot about the size of a half dollar near the base of her spine. That spot, she told me, was a source of grinding pain. And when we compared notes the next evening, the long stripe I'd seen on her back covered the length of the pain she feels every day.

For three nights we did the massages. Each following day we noted comparisons. Then she returned to the physical therapist for the second appointment. Surprised at Jul's progress, the therapist cut the planned number of sessions in half.

I wish I could say my partner is cured, but she isn't. Her pain never completely vanished and intermittently worsens. We have not sustained the massage experiment either. On my part, transmitting the healing energy seems to require a clear mind without thoughts, and I'm not currently able to sustain this state for long periods of time on a consistent basis. Nor am I sure how to work with this energy, or even if I can over an extended period.

In time, I'm certain I'll know this energy's purpose in my life, and how to use it, if I'm to do so. At this point, what's important for me to take from this experience is the realization that we use so little of what we're capable of, and know so little about who we are. To find out, we must be open to possibility and take the time to let our talents emerge.

The World

Is More

Than We Know

Many years ago, my friend's son was exploring his college career options. When he considered majoring in Astrophysics, his mother advised him, "Instead of outer space, why not study inner space?" She was referring not to the psyche, but to the inner realms, the spiritual plane that escapes our awareness and eludes our investigative methods.

For the most part, we believe the world is what we can see. The invisible energy flying around us, like radio waves, microwaves, sonar, and even the wind, we believe in because we see its effects. Similarly, physicists discover unknown facets of the universe by noticing effects on existing objects that they can't explain by known phenomena. In understanding and explaining the non-physical world, we have not seriously considered this possibility. What if unseen phenomena exist that affect our lives but we are not aware? And how would we know to look for those phenomena if we haven't even noticed the effects? Or, what if the effects are erroneously attributed to known phenomena and are no longer questioned?

Our expectations and beliefs limit what we can know and see. Our minds are so busy, and so full of formal and informal learning, that it's difficult to simply observe, without automatically applying labels, rules, emotions, or value judgments to what we see. To assure our comfort, make it easier to manage information, or just out of habit—because it's the way we've been taught—we try to make experiences and observations fit into our existing mental constructions and perspectives. If an experience won't fit, we frequently find ways to ignore, deny, or forget it. Rarely are we willing to modify our constructions or try to view life without these aids.

During the two years of writing this book, I've tried to simply observe and record rather than fit what I see into an existing structure, system, or faith tradition. I've tried to be open, expecting nothing, and yet accepting of new insights and experiences as they appear. I've tried to be alert, and notice when I was wrapping a paradigm around a new experience, rather than just seeing without classifying or judging.

This openness, I've found, is nothing to fear. In fact, in this state of mind, I feel calmer, more at ease. My mind doesn't need to grope for explanations or dig through my 40-year-old mental library to find an applicable reference. In this stillness, the vast expansiveness of our universe feels like home. In this state, other layers of existence emerge into consciousness. Through this emergence, I've come to accept that our world is so much more than we know, and so much more than we can understand or communicate using existing methods and tools.

BETWEEN TWO WORLDS

IN WESTERN CULTURE, we believe the physical world is the only world, or that other worlds exist but are separate, unreachable and uninhabited. Western consciousness is limited in that way. But the increasing complexity of our world is forcing expanded consciousness, and expanded consciousness, in turn, will allow us to see and experience other dimensions, if we look closely enough.

Last year, I attended a weekend spiritual retreat in the Cascade Mountains. Restless and not much interested in the afternoon meditation session, I instead browsed the downstairs library. My fingers moved across the spines, nothing new, nothing new, nothing new... ahhh...what's this? *Playing Ball on Running Water.*

The title leaped out at me the way symbols and objects in our environment do when there's a message or meaning that's important for us. One of the experiences that has pushed me to write this book is that I have no interest in reading. I even experience repulsion toward it at times. In the past, the book's subject would have interested me. But on this day, the title's metaphor was the message.

Playing Ball on Running Water. This is the way the physical world and the spiritual world interact. While we are playing ball in the physical world, the unseen world is moving beneath our feet (and all around us). We know the rules of the ball game. We can see the pitches and the players and anticipate the moves. We know how to keep score, and what the score is. What we don't know is what the currents below us conceal, the speed or direction of their movement, how deep or powerful they are, and if or when that might change. We may not even know this running water exists and so are surprised when suddenly the field shifts and we're facing a tidal wave or feel ourselves getting sucked into an eddy.

Life is a web of simultaneous actions, processes, dimensions, currents, and strands of different heights, lengths, thicknesses, textures, vibrations, and frequency levels. We live in only a small part of this web, but we're influenced by its incalculable gyrations. Some we're conscious of and some we're not. Some we can anticipate and some we can't. Our consciousness shows us only so much, gives us certain knowledge and allows us to anticipate and see a certain distance around ourselves. We won't know what distant actions or objects—those out of our field of vision or awareness—are affecting us. We don't even know they exist or to look for them. Yet we may experience the effects.

The more open to this process we become, the more consciously aware and spirit-guided we are, the more our field of vision or sensing expands. It's why, when we act intuitively, we end up in the right place or time. Intuition can see, grasp and instantly compute the complexity our cognition can't contain or process.

There are people whose consciousness can shift from one world to the other, and people who draw on multiple worlds but whose focus, attention, or perspective are predominately in the physical. They are able to understand and intervene in non-physical dimensions. Sometimes they can communicate knowledge or messages from those realms to humans in the physical plane. But in Western culture, usually we don't believe in this consciousness shifting capability and possess limited language to talk about or describe it, making communicating difficult. Consciousness shifters, though, even without communicating directly what they know, have access to a wider range of knowledge and information by which to make decisions or take action.

We all have this capacity to varying degrees but most of us are completely unaware of it. We have not explored deeply enough, nor have we paid attention when those realms rise up around us. Attachment to and focus on the physical blinds us to other dimensions and our ability to interact with them. When our bodies shut down, or we intentionally shift our focus, we can see these worlds and know that they're not as separate or distant as we think.

Dying is prime time for experiencing this mingling of worlds.

Sometimes the dead put a foot in our world to offer advice, information, comfort, or encouragement. When an author acquaintance was working on her first book, she smelled her deceased father's pipe tobacco in the room and knew he was cheering her on. It works the other way too. Sometimes a dying person can see what awaits them when they surrender the physical.

Our worlds are converging. As we manipulate and change the physical world, the boundaries between the realms become less clear. For now, most of us still need extreme circumstances, like death, to illuminate this convergence. Eventually, as we open ourselves to spirit and allow our consciousness to expand, we will perceive and understand the overlap and learn to navigate in blended worlds.

KILLING TIME

IN THE TWILIGHT MORNING, when I've finished my chores and the world has sleep in its eyes, I listen to those calls in the stillness, the crackling branches emitting invisible cheeps and twitters, the squawk and natter of the crows, the staccato bleating of a baby sea lion and its big brother's honking reply.

It's been a long year and a short year, this year after my best friend died. Clocks and calendars, they sit on time, ignoring the undulations, suppressing the heaving, floating over the crevices, convincing us that the days move smoothly, in measured steps, predictable, logical, incremental. Convincing us that time exists.

Instead of a tool that helps us navigate the logistics of large-scale interaction, mass production and transport, we've come to believe that time itself is a natural aspect of life. We've accepted the illusion of time. Made it reality. Structured our existence by it. We go against our own body's rhythms, against seasonal changes, clog up our roadways, and develop cultural understandings about how rigid we're to follow these metered measures, all to keep the march of time.

But I've noticed this year, in my morning solitude, that time is elastic. It expands and contracts. Like those days when I think it's Friday but it's only Wednesday, and those days when Friday shows up before I've had a chance to settle into mid-week. Often, when I feel this way, others around me do too. In a crisis or while concentrating, time slows down, and when we're aging, or having fun, it passes all too quickly.

These glimpses are the natural state of time penetrating our cultural overlay. Natural time is flexible and flowing and dependent on a confluence of energies, or circumstances and actions, to bring things into being. In cultural time, we share beliefs about how many days, or months or years it should take to accomplish a specific goal, about how quickly or slowly change can happen, or the incremental, structured set of steps required to effect change or reach goals. When we're traveling in natural time, things we expect to take years can happen instantly and vice versa. People we never knew or even thought about meeting can suddenly show up in our life. Opportunities arise unanticipated and from unlikely places and we will often find ourselves in the right place at the right time.

Synchronicity, serendipity, and deja vu are manifestations of natural time. They happen when they happen, not on our schedule. Our recognition of this natural time flow and yet inability to direct and manipulate it, can produce anxiety and cause us to resist, ignore or deny it. Or we can revel in its mystery and surprise. When our delight in discovery outweighs our fear, we'll be able to go where natural time takes us.

WE ARE NOT ALONE

MANY YEARS AGO, I remember listening to a couple of people at a spiritual gathering describing the energies they saw in the room and in the woods outside the window while we waited for a channeling session to start. I thought, *uhmm, hmmm.* I was attending the channeling session out of curiosity. Working at a mental health clinic, I wanted to know if there was any difference between what I was about to witness and the hallucinations and delusions we medicated every day. I've been skeptical about the fairy world, angels, aliens, and other realms, not necessarily disbelieving their existence, but certainly reserving my right to decide that this is a ridiculous concoction of the fantasy-prone.

Early last year, sitting on our deck, which overlooks dense trees and vegetation down the hill to Puget Sound, I noticed energy patches, transparent reddish/pink, blue and green, like flat balls or bubbles just floating around. Some, mostly the green and blue ones, stayed close to the tree branches. The reddish ones skipped and danced just above the water. All of them were approximately the same size, 18-inch diameter disks. *Ahhh, reflected sunlight*, I figured. Nope, they showed up several more times, even when the sun wasn't out. When I came home from work one day, trees in our neighbor's yard were being cut down and these energy patches, which I now know as nature spirits, were frantically flying in all directions.

I don't see these beings often, yet I've begun to see others in different shapes, with varying movements and colors, and sizes—including one huge gray/black one shaped like a puffy manta ray. From my living room, I calmly watched it, watching me through the sliding glass door. It didn't scare me until it went away and I began questioning what it was and why it was outside my window.

This being was big and dark. Ominous, my social conditioning told me. So I started thinking it must be a bad omen. *What was going on in my life that could go wrong? Whom do I love who might be in trouble?* My anxiety spiked as the irrational thoughts flashed faster. Then I grabbed hold of objectivity and reason. While I was watching this being, without thought, it didn't feel threatening at all. If its intent was warning, or if it was a menace, my spirit would have sensed that energy. This being just exists, I realized. Just like me.

I've come to accept that I'm seeing, literally with my eyes, other realms of existence and deeper levels of being. Sitting on our deck talking with friends one day, I looked across the Sound at the Olympic

Mountains and saw, rising out of one of the large peaks what I at first thought was volcanic steam. Then I realized it was more like a pear-shaped cloud, gently rising, floating almost. This time, I silently questioned without skepticism, and knew that it was the mountain's soul. Perhaps this is why I'm beginning to see these invisible energies, so I'll believe. So I'll know without doubt that the world we live in is not ours alone. That what we do in it and to it affects more than human life.

HERE, THERE, OR EVERYWHERE?

MY TOES GRIPPED THE FAMILIAR COBBLESTONES as I plodded barefoot up the steep streets of a mountain town. Entering a small shop, I saw its haphazard inventory scattered across a rough, bare, board floor and walls. I didn't need to duck or sway to miss the utensils, netting, and tools hanging from a low ceiling beam, nor sidestep the dusty brown cloth sacks slumped in corners and flopped over precariously stacked wooden boxes and barrels. The items I came for were near the door, in clear jars, like old apothecary jars. My purchase was calculated and recorded on a tool similar to an abacus, with strands of beads of varying colors representing designated amounts.

This experience happened while I slept, but it felt solid, beyond a dream and beyond symbolic. I was *in* this town. I don't know how or why I visited this village, assuming that I was a visitor, rather than a native. I didn't see my own body, nor do I recall the physical appearance of the shopkeeper. Perhaps I was in this store in spirit only, my consciousness traveling between this life and another. If so, did I connect to or drop into the consciousness of another? Or might this be a simultaneous existence? Perhaps we're like an octopus. Each tentacle would be a unique existence, another dimension of self that is connected to and springs from the source—metaphorically the octopus trunk, literally the universe, the life force, the All Knowingness, or God, whatever label we choose to apply.

In a few instances, people have told me that they recognize me. Not because they saw me at an event or in a photograph, but from a deeper level of recognition, perhaps a past life connection. When people have said this to me and I didn't feel a reciprocal recognition (which is usually the case), their admission made me wary of them. I rarely instantaneously recognize people. When I do, I don't know the details of our connection, so I keep quiet about my knowing and wait to see if this recognition becomes important in any way.

Only once did I recognize a person at this deep level and simultaneously know any details of the connection. This recognition happened with a long-time friend, rather than a new acquaintance. While Mark and I cooked breakfast together one morning, I saw a flash image in my mind of me as a man on a horse dressed in medieval battle gear. In the image, I saw Mark as a young woman filled with sorrow standing before me. She was either my sister or my lover. I couldn't determine which. I just sensed the strong loving bonds between us. This woman was afraid I would die in battle and begged me to stay.

Earlier that day, we had talked and wept together. We both knew that my leaving could not be foregone, regardless of its outcome.

In other instantaneous recognition experiences, I was not aware of the specific relationship or circumstances, only the feeling. Usually this feeling is a powerful attraction or repulsion. Pheromones? Maybe. But the feeling usually does not translate as sexual. It translates as familiarity. I once felt this negative recognition with a person I would have to work with for a long time, so I tried to blow off the knowing. I focused on the woman's strengths and kindnesses, hoping they would wash away my discomfort with her. I watched her behavior, searching for anything that might be leading me to this wariness. Nothing. This residue was from another place, or time, or existence.

When I was in my twenties, an experience made me wonder if we can, or do, simultaneously exist as more than one life form. In a dream, I watched a purple swan glide away from me across a lake, moonlight illuminating the rippling trail that fanned out at my feet. The swan was me. Yet I also stood on the bank in human form, aware that I was watching myself swim. This dual existence felt solid and natural, an experience that sparked neither questioning nor awe.

I told no one about this dream. The next day, one of the members of a spiritual group I belonged to handed me a birthday card. On the cover was a glowing purple swan. Coincidence? Perhaps. But it was the kind of coincidence that made me shiver. It was not my birthday, nor did he sign the card. He gave it to me, he said, because of the swan. Inside, it read, "May beauty always touch your life as beautifully as you have touched mine." I have no idea if purple swans exist somewhere, but it felt like this communication was between the swan and me, our lives touching. The person delivering the card was simply a mediary providing confirmation of an experience that was otherwise too bizarre for me to believe.

The common state in all of these fleeting recognitions is their solidity, subtle, yet firm. I don't know where the "dream" mountain village is located, maybe the Himalayas or Andes. But if the physical body and mind that sits writing this book ever finds itself in this village, I'll know it was the village I visited during my midnight ride. And if I ever see a purple swan ... I'll remember our connection and the beauty of my moonlight swim.

Living

From Spirit

From a logical standpoint, publishing *Natural Urges* before writing a book about death and dying makes no sense. After many years of research, writing, presentations, and media interviews, I have some expertise in the funeral field on which to draw for marketing. But I have never written, taught, or spoken publicly about spirituality. Given this nonsensical flip-flop, and my general resistance to exposing my spiritual self in writing, I figured the answer was to write both books simultaneously. That plan worked for a year, then the death and dying material stopped flowing. All I could produce were essays for *Natural Urges*.

Living from spirit, I've found, is not a process we control. We make the choice to do it or not, to follow its guidance or not, but we don't direct what it brings us, where it takes us, or how or when. Which is not to say all life is scripted or that we have no responsibility for our actions. It isn't, and we do. Spirit is not external to us. It's part of who we are. At times, spirit takes the lead. Other times our ego, emotions, or body motivates our actions, but always the responsibility belongs to us.

Spirit moves at its own pace and rhythm, a rhythm that's unique in each of us, and can change over time. Sometimes I experience extremely active periods, times when my spirit prods me constantly, delivering numerous insights, or compelling me to action. I'm zooming ahead. Everything is falling into place. I'm in the zone. Then suddenly the ground caves in, or I'm jerked back to the starting line, maybe even behind it. Nothing makes sense. I'm lost in the morass. In this state, I even feel like the connection is lost. From experience, though, I know it isn't.

Racing, dragging, resting, changing course, taking a new mode of transportation, or landing on unfamiliar terrain, it's the spirit's way. That makes the process suspicious in Western culture, where predictability and order are king, and it creates uncertainty and doubt in those of us who experience it—until we accept the nature of spirit and learn to trust it. When we do, the ups and downs and confusion can settle into a clear, steady state of broadened awareness, a settled knowing in which we feel our spirit's presence simply as calm assurance and inner strength.

To let our spirit guide us, we have to sense its pace, feel its fluctuations, respond when necessary and wait when not. Living in the universal flow requires letting our resistance melt away, letting go of our fear and our ego's need for control. I've been attuned to my spirit's voice all my life, but now I'm learning to live with this part of the process. As much as I might like to put spiritual guidance in a straitjacket and haul it around, I can't. My spirit won't allow it. Besides, in surrendering, I'm rewarded with a beauty and majesty in life I otherwise can't see.

RIDING THE WAVES

A FILE CARD REMINDER NOTE tacked to the wall over my desk reads: "Life's a journey. Enjoy the ride." I'm an achiever. No task is too big for me to take on. I'll juggle half a dozen major projects simultaneously and do them all reasonably well. Our action-oriented, multitasking Western culture rewards this kind of behavior so I need a counterbalance, a prompter to remind me that my spirit operates on a slower, less deliberate pace.

Living at American society's speed is like taking a cross-country train trip and never looking out the window (unless it's to count the mileposts), only jumping up and smiling when the destination is in sight. As we're pulling into the station, we're standing at the door with our bags, itching to jump off before we've stopped, hungry to explore the new venue. Then, while we're scouting the territory, we're thinking about our next destination and how we'll get there.

But I've found that the journey is the ride. Destinations are stops along the way where we can relax, reflect, and explore deeper, but our spirit's revelations spring from the things we do everyday, the people we meet and observe and talk with, seeing events or objects or patterns we didn't anticipate, or experiencing the routine in a new way. Moments of awe don't come when we're seeking them. They show up unexpectedly, when we're listening deeply and opening ourselves to life's currents. Lessons can appear in the least likely circumstances, in places we believed not conducive, and from people we may think could never teach us anything.

On a Saturday morning, my partner and I walked along familiar Seattle streets and stopped at a coffee shop we visit often. Leaving the shop, I was talking and starting to sip my coffee when I felt the paper cup vibrate, saw the tiny liquid waves inside, and noticed vibrations in my chest. Undoubtedly, this sound energy hitting the cup and bouncing back at me happened before, but I never paid attention. Now I notice other forms of unseen energy in our world.

Waiting, too, is part of the ride, a difficult part for someone who prefers to go full throttle with projects and plans. A year before my partner and I moved to Seattle, we simultaneously, intuitively sensed that our life was going to change dramatically, but we couldn't tell when that would happen, or what it would involve. The impending change felt neither positive nor negative, just open-ended. This state of suspension underlying our daily routine continued so long without either of us getting any hints about the outcome that we developed a laughing, shoulder-shrugging mantra, "You just never know."

As I started writing *Natural Urges*, my intuition told me to get a progressed astrological chart reading. In my teen and twenties searching years, I spent three months teaching myself to calculate and interpret charts, trying to determine for myself if this tool was useful or a bunch of hooey. Even though I landed on the side of astrology, I've not sought readings often. But my confidence was sagging as I began this writing project, so I went. The astrologer's reading confirmed the major themes and directions in my life, and she advised me to slow down and allow all that I know to emerge. "You'll be ready when the time is right," she said.

From my perspective, I had already slowed to a near halt. I was spending many mornings and evenings mindlessly sitting on our deck. Most weekends, I did the same, if I wasn't writing or maintaining my web sites. "But I'm ready now," I protested, knowing the rebellion was useless.

"Maybe you are, but the universe isn't ready for you yet!" she said, laughing at the impatience written all over my body, and my chart. Nothing we do, I've learned, will hurry or slow the pace of the universe. So we might as well relax and soak up the present.

A friend told me a beautiful story about the kind of receptivity needed to hear our spirit's voice. When Rebecca was five years old, she played in the ocean's edges while her nine-month pregnant mother sat on the beach reading and watching her daughter. After a while, Rebecca drifted so far into the surf that she could no longer resist the current and keep her feet on the sand. Neither could she swim. Saltwater burned her nose as she struggled, screaming and chopping the water. Her mother, afraid to wade in, demanded Rebecca stop fighting and float. When she did, the waves carried her to shore.

WAYS OF KNOWING

THERE ARE MANY WAYS OF KNOWING. The key is to use the right method at the right time, and for the right purpose. Skyscrapers, bridges, and computers would never be built if we were incapable of logic. Art would never be produced if we couldn't extract the knowledge of emotion or tap our intuition. Our body's physicality tells us what it needs to be healthy. For spiritual knowledge, we must be receptive to the nuances of other dimensions.

The universe works through all of these methods, but our culture doesn't support or value all of them, especially not in the same person. Living whole requires drawing on all of these ways of knowing and using them as crosschecks to temper each other. We need our intellectual, rational capacity to gauge belief, so we don't fall prey to fundamentalism, dogma, and unquestioning assumptions. We must get out of our head and into our body to learn to feel and interpret its subtle messages and regain its wisdom. We need to match our experiences, feelings, and knowledge with what we're told by our culture, and determine if there's a gap. To let our spirit's language emerge, we have to carve new paths and open new channels.

For most of us, spirit is multilingual. It uses signs, symbols, colors, tactile and visual impressions, dreams, intuition, body sensations, or any combination of methods. We may be more receptive to one language than another, and that may change with circumstances, or time, or our growth.

Sometimes dreams predominate, at other times bodily sensations prevail, or signs in the natural world. Some people interpret symbols, or see luminosity and meaning in what for most of us are ordinary objects or events. They record simple, unnoticeable, otherwise forgettable interactions and draw essential insights out of them. Spirit uses whatever tools it needs to be recognized. If the message is urgent enough, it will be delivered over and over again in many forms until we hear and accept it.

Feeling and following our spirit's traveling speed requires sensing deeply, allowing our body to respond subtly, without words. In our quest to discipline and distance ourselves from our own flesh, we have nearly lost touch with this direct form of spirit communication. Our body resonates to our spirit's pulse, and the pulse of our planet. Listening to and trusting our body keeps it healthy, and lets us dance our spirit's dance.

Tuning into our spirit's voice and interpreting the language it uses is essential to living from spirit. Silence and stillness are its medium.

We need periodic places of rest, of quiet and solitude, especially when we're learning to listen to our spirit. When we're solidly connected to it, and have learned to carry silence and stillness inside us, we can hear and respond to spirit even in chaotic, noisy external environments. Yet we need the occasional respite and rejuvenation of a serene environment to assure that we stay connected and perceive without distortion.

As increasing numbers of us travel along this road, we will relearn the spirit's lost language and develop new ways of knowing. There are teachers among us, those who know and whose purpose is to spread the language. As our personal-social-cultural transformation unwinds, their presence will be more widely known. There are tools that can help solidify our connection to spirit, like meditation, prayer, and exercises, and we should use them as needed. But basically, hearing our spirit's voice is about opening up, about allowing ourselves to believe our own experience and to explore it for its meaning, truth and guidance. It's about coming to trust what we know and feel, the insights we're given, and to be aware of, and act on when appropriate, ever subtler communications.

As consciousness expands, all of our ways of knowing will be necessary. As will discernment, the ability to weigh the communication or information received against the soul's truth reflector, against our own knowledge and experience, and the external environment. With this testing, which sometimes takes seconds, and sometimes years, clarity rises and spotlights the kernel of truth.

DISCOVERING MEANING

When I was in my teens, I tried one day to see my aura. I squinted at the mirror, narrowed my eyes, stared at the center of my forehead. Nothing. I leaned closer, blocking out the walls behind and beside me, shrinking my focus. A thin, silver lining arched a half-inch above my head. Long blue-purple pulses flickered at their ends, dancing like flames. Time stopped, letting me watch in awe.

Where did this come from? With my first question the light vanished. So I tried to bring it back. I squinted. I squeezed. I crossed my eyes and pushed my nose right up against the mirror, but it wouldn't show itself. If I saw it once, I should be able to see it again, I reasoned. Then I heard that little voice of recognition, the silent voice that hammers home truths. "If you saw it once and you don't believe it, you won't believe it if you see it a second time or a third time."

But I'm a scientist, I say, fending off the chastisement. I need validation. Reliability. Repetition is the only way to be sure. With this little voice, though, there's no argument. I can feel its shrugged shoulders. I can either accept it, or not. It sheds no tears either way. My heart accepts it. My mind refuses.

The answer to this dilemma is to go with my heart and let my mind follow. Instead of searching for proof that an experience is real, I should trust the experience, accept its authenticity, and ask instead what it means for me. Is this an experience from which there is something to be learned or something I should know?

If your mind is like mine, used to being in charge, it won't be happy about this new arrangement. Taming its resistance will take a while. Once the mind settles into this way of questioning, it will realize that it's not being silenced, just refocused and used to understand the world in a different way. Which doesn't mean it will never again protest its dethroning. It will. Especially during those times when its filtering isn't needed—when the message, meaning, or insight is immediately known and understood. That's when the logical mind's rebellion tries to produce doubt and undermine spirit's communication.

Our world and our lives brim with meaning. It's all around us. Yet the interpretation is unique to each of us—how we arrive at it and what that meaning is. Three of us might see the same object or event, or hear the same music, but each of us may take away our own meaning or experience of it. Some might find no meaning at all. The event or object, if noticed, is merely an amusement or ordinary occurrence, easily forgotten.

This winter, a single purple flower bloomed in our yard. To me, it signaled being ahead of the crowd, and growing despite harsh conditions. I didn't mention this flower or its symbolism until the next day, when it snowed. Then, when I pointed to it, my friend just thought it was an oddity. When I told her what it meant to me, she laughed and told me what it meant to her. "Sometimes it doesn't pay to be ahead of the pack."

Often the meaning we intuit will not be clear to others, and may even be nonsensical to them if we attempt to explain it. Once I wrote a paper for a class in which I described one of my favorite activities, sitting by a stream watching the water flow. Tiny twigs and leaves rode the swirls, dunked and bobbed and swam with the current. A small styrofoam cup ran into a partially submerged branch. The cup waved and wagged but couldn't free itself from the snarl. The water flowed around it, leaving it stuck. Eventually, it began to rain. The drops agitated the branch and the current enough to set the gyrating cup sailing. "Like life," I wrote, "sometimes you run into an obstacle and all your struggling isn't enough. Sometimes you have to wait for the circumstances to change." My instructor wrote in the margin, "Huh?"

These kinds of events, meanings and misunderstandings are mild. Basically, they're symbolic and symbolism is understood in our culture, even if the interpretations aren't widely shared. People who see energy, hear voices, or intuit the presence of other life forms often aren't even believed, and there's not much language to help explain. Trying to use words in our Western lexicon to convey a direct experience that isn't even understood in our culture trumps trying to describe a piece of art or a wine or a smell. Because it's worked for me, I'll offer a little word of advice: Keep a sense of humor.

What matters is whether the meaning resonates in us. Whether, in our core, it feels true for us. It may not be true for others. That's why only we can interpret our own dreams. Even if some of the symbols are common in our culture, they may carry a unique message for the dreamer. The symbols may feel altered by their context, or sequence, or juxtaposition to other symbols. In the same dream, some images or insights may be literal and some figurative. Only the dreamer can sense these subtle twists and distinctions and ascertain their meaning.

Learning to trust our own experience and divine its meaning, rather than search for proof of its existence or reality, is an art. Like drawing, dancing, writing, or playing an instrument, there are a few key components and techniques to be learned. But eventually the artist submerges technique and flies with the wind.

CLEAR AS A CRYSTAL BELL

DRIVING NORTH ON INTERSTATE 5 to a Saturday morning conference, I memorized the exit number to get to the retreat center. Then my mind switched to autopilot. *How can we tell when a message or insight is truly from the spirit?* I wondered. *How do we know when it's a product of mental or environmental distortion, or ego needs or desires...?*

Suddenly, I snapped to attention and spotted exit 221. *That's my exit. Or is it?* I had a vague feeling that I'd passed my exit already. Was it 221, or 212? The more I questioned it, the less certain I was. Then I reasoned, it must be 221. Surely it was my intuition that woke me from my reverie just as I reached the place where I needed to turn.

I waited for that sterling certainty that accompanies intuitive knowledge, but it didn't emerge. What to do? I was running late. The conference was scheduled to start in fifteen minutes and I still had to travel five miles to the retreat center after leaving the freeway. Sitting at the crossroad, trying to decide which way to go, and whether finding myself at this intersection was an intuitive aid or a not-paying-attention mistake, I heard, "If it's intuition, you *know* immediately. If you can't decide, assume it's reason and follow it." I turned back toward the exit I'd missed and pulled into the conference center right on time.

Intuition, I find, is easy to confuse with the ego's wishes. With intuition, we see no external signs, usually no body messages or visions. It's pure knowing. So it's crucial to develop a method of gauging whether the information we receive is tangled up with and distorted by what we want to believe or what our ego wants.

Intuition lays out the unvarnished truth, but the many filters we acquire for living in this world can twist our reception and lead us astray. In trying to decide if my intuition was guiding me to the right exit, I wasn't listening objectively. I wanted to believe that my intuition would so protect and guide me that I could drive blind, without paying attention to the landmarks or putting any effort in myself. It doesn't work that way. Believing that it does can lead us along some weird and destructive paths.

To receive unadulterated intuitive knowledge (and by the way, no other kind is worth receiving), I need to be a clear channel, like a crystal bell, where no blockages of any sort distort the information. Sometimes, this requires body clarity, purifying, exercising, healing or an array of physical cleansings.

Mostly, at least for me, it's a mind thing, a mental Spring cleaning.

It's a continuous process of *unlearning*, of scouring and eliminating unconsciously held assumptions, unexamined beliefs, and unrealistic expectations. This cleansing requires letting go of old, lingering hurts and resentments. Recognizing the cultural lenses that bend and shape my perceptions is imperative. I must toss out arbitrary shoulds and shouldn'ts, and anything that skews my ability to accept intuitive knowledge without bias, anything that might divert or subvert this subtle communication and my ability to perceive it clearly. I've used this technique most of my life. Still, I live in a world filled with lenses, so some days are cloudy.

WHY KNOW?

FOR ME, PREMONITIONS ARE RARE, and often banal. A waylaid snatch from the collective unconscious. A peek at the footnotes of the Akashic Record, the medium that contains all thoughts and actions. Perhaps a helpful but less than earth-shaking shard of knowledge.

Driving around north Houston one afternoon, just wasting time, I stopped at a fork in the road. One path led out of town, the other toward my central city home. I turned the wheel away, then felt I should go home. *The UPS man is coming.* Stupid thought! I wasn't expecting a package. But I wasn't committed to more ambling either, so I drove home. Before I even made it to the bathroom, a courier driver knocked on the door. The delivery was for my mother. Since I lived in a neighborhood where any package left outside wouldn't stay long, this message, although hardly earth-shattering, wasn't so ridiculous after all.

But the first premonition I recall is far from trivial, and forever linked in my memory with my great-grandmother. She lived across Highway 61 from my parents' Missouri farm. As a pre-schooler, I spent long days with her, feeding the chickens, playing in the hayloft while she fed the cows, licking cookie dough off her wooden spatula, and rummaging through her crate of nylon loops that we'd tie together so I could crochet crooked potholders. In the afternoon, while the bread was rising and clothes were drying on the line, she sat in her rocker by the living room window reading her tattered German bible.

Afternoons were my favorite time with her. I'd crawl into the rocking chair next to hers, she'd hand me a cracked leather hymnal I was too young to read, and we'd sing, the sunshine pouring in the window, like Jesus standing behind us, his hands on our shoulders, singing along.

When I was nine years old, Grandma fell, broke her hip and ended up in the hospital. Children weren't allowed to visit patients in those 1960s days, at least not in the rural Midwest. Even when my mom spent weeks inside those sanitary walls after her surgeries, my brother and sister and I stayed home or waited in the lobby. One morning when mom was going to visit my grandmother, I pleaded with her to let me go.

"Grandma's going to die," I told her. She laughed and assured me that grandma would be home in a few days and that I could go see her as soon as she left the hospital. "No," I insisted, "I won't get to see her. She's going to die."

Out of patience, my mother stomped out to the driveway leaving me behind screaming, demanding that she take me along. Despite kicking and banging the car door with my fists, I wasn't allowed to go, and my mother drove away. So I curled up in bed, my head beneath the blankets, and cried myself to sleep. When I woke up, mom was sitting beside me. My grandmother had contracted pneumonia, then her heart failed. She died suddenly. I've not been fond of premonitions since. Perhaps that's why they don't come around often.

My friend Juanita experienced frequent premonitions as a child. Telling others about them often got her in trouble, so she learned to be silent. As an adult, she tried to ignore her premonitions because they frightened and worried her, and there was nothing she could do to change the outcome. Juanita's childhood premonitions varied in content. But in her adult premonitions, she usually saw impending accidents, trains, cars, planes, or murders, but not in enough detail to identify the victims or to intervene.

Even if we see the details, I don't know whether we can intervene when premonitions notify us, or if we should. Probably, like most things, it depends. As in routine daily life, knowledge carries with it the responsibility of discernment—the requirement to judge, not in the sense of good or bad but whether and how to act on the information. American society, so steeped in privacy and individual rights and freedoms, makes it easy to err by omission. When we don't want to get in anybody's business, don't want to tell anybody what to do, don't want to be told what to do, and want everybody to just live and let live, then it can be difficult to determine when we have some responsibility to act and when we should leave people and events alone.

Finding this balance is a challenge. It takes wisdom to realize when to act, and when to just sit with the knowing. Sometimes it's necessary to simply reflect on our awareness or open ourselves to the experience without trying to control it.

Less than a year after I'd stashed my unpublished book and decided to get away from this spirituality stuff, my friend Juanita's 16-year-old son, Jeremy, drowned. Two nights before, I had dreamed of a scroll filled with names, its bottom half shrouded in mist and all the names illegible except the one that rolled over the top and vanished in the clouds until it came round again. The visible name was Juanita Warren, my friend's maiden name. This dream repeated all night. Over and over. No embellishments in its retelling. Just the retelling.

Not only was this dream unusual in its intense focus and repetition, it was unusual too because Juanita and I had parted in anger nearly two years earlier. Despite the disruption in our friendship, when I woke up, I made a mental note to call, but got busy with daily tasks, and forgot.

That night, I dreamed all night of chaos, darkness, crowds and running. I couldn't distinguish figures or faces, just pandemonium. Again, this scene repeated, over and over. Burning itself into my consciousness. I knew it was associated with Juanita. That morning,

Natural Urges

I taped a reminder note on the refrigerator to call her after work. When I got home, my phone rang instead. A mutual friend told me that Juanita's son drowned that day. His brother had tried to pull him out of the pond and back into the boat, without success.

I've questioned my actions, or inaction, around these dreams often. Jeremy died at a time when I was trying to ignore and deny that I know what I know of the spiritual world. If only I had paid more attention to the dreams. If only I had done...what? Nothing in my dream told me that Jeremy would die. The dreams weren't even about Jeremy. They focused on his mother. If I had phoned before Jeremy died, what would I have said? And if I had relayed the dreams, what would such vagueness have changed?

Perhaps that's why the specifics of precognitive knowing often remain shadowy. So we can't try to reverse the course of what's to come. In general, we're not very good at sitting with pain—our own or that of others. Yet at times sitting with it, letting it be, is exactly the action that's needed. Perhaps precognitive knowing will occur more often and in more detail when we develop this mastery. But then again, would we want it to?

I couldn't have stopped Jeremy's drowning. Some people know the day they will die. I think Jeremy knew. He was sensitive, compassionate, highly intuitive, and curious about his purpose on earth. He was his mother's favorite child. Juanita never tried to hide her preference, so everyone knew she cherished Jeremy. During one of the last times I talked with him, he was exploring numerology. Knowing that I had studied the subject, Jeremy asked me to calculate his chart. It was filled with Master numbers—indicating this young man was an old, old soul.

Why he was born, and why he died so soon, I don't know. But I believe his spirit was alerting me in my dreams to prepare me for comforting and supporting his mother in her overwhelming grief. Juanita had many friends and family members, so had I not experienced our connection in these dreams, I would have believed I was neither needed nor welcome at Jeremy's funeral. Nor would I have been with her to read the signs Jeremy sent after his death.

Signs are a way of knowing and communicating that takes a limitless variety of forms. A song lyric, a book title, water's ripple pattern, a street name, a fluttering leaf, a candle flame, goose bumps, headaches, an overheard snippet of conversation, an unusual juxtaposition of objects, even a smell. Whatever the shape, texture, or presentation, the common characteristic is luminescence, a subtle energy that attracts the interpreter's attention at the spirit level, not the cognitive level.

A charge that doubters raise goes something like this. "Yeah, sure, out of all the stars in the sky and all the people on this planet, that star appeared just for you, uh huh!" It's a reasonable doubt. It's just wrong. Signs can appear only to an individual, and only momentarily. But when signs are objects that exist in our environment, they don't show up solely for the sake of an individual. Any observer can see these objects. They become signs for anyone who conveys or receives meaning or information through or from them in pure energy form. To other people, these objects are only what they are physically.

The night of Jeremy's wake, Juanita and I stood in silence outside the funeral home while she smoked a cigarette. Above us, a red star blinked. I sensed it was a sign from Jeremy letting us know that he was OK. Jeremy wanted me to tell his mother, for solace. No way was I going to do that! Juanita and I disagreed before about premonitions and intuitive knowledge and I knew she was closed to the subject. So was I, I thought. Besides, this woman was grieving every parent's worst fear. I wasn't about to say something that I wasn't sure I believed and that I knew she wouldn't. But Jeremy persisted. So I told Juanita that he was OK.

Always the cross-examiner, Juanita asked, "How do you know?" I cringed. I'd hoped she'd just accept the intended comfort.

I pointed at the red star. "Because he's saying so." She glanced briefly at the cool, dark sky, scowled at me, then stubbed her cigarette out on the brick facade and walked inside.

So I never mentioned the sharp breeze that rose out of that hot, still, sunny day when we lowered Jeremy's body into the ground, and died away as we left the cemetery, or the double rainbow that spread over Jeremy's family's house after his funeral. Jeremy was smiling, happy that I recognized him, but sad, wishing he could penetrate his mother's resistance and ease her grief.

MAIN ATTRACTIONS

Paying attention to the material objects we're attracted to can clue us in to spiritual needs. So can objects in our natural world. These objects possess energy of their own, as well as symbolic energy. This energy can be exchanged, shared, integrated, dissipated, and used to facilitate growth, change, or balance in our being or our environment.

When I was in my late 20s, I wore a single, white feather that dangled from my right earlobe and lay on my shoulder. Everyone noticed. It's difficult to miss an eight-inch long earring on a nearly six-foot tall, 200-pound woman. Yet the feather meant different things to different people. An animal-rights guy blasted me for murdering a bird and being crass enough to tout my kill. Some people assumed I'm Native American. Others read the feather as the sign of a free spirit, a cool, hippie type. Many just thought I was odd. In five years of wearing that feather, only one person ever guessed my true motive and asked me about it.

I liked the earring's look: the wildness, the whiteness, mixed with my unruly, waist-length mahogany hair. When I wore it with my business suit, I savored the visual contradiction. But this white feather resonated with me because of its spiritual energy and symbolism.

I began wearing the earring after I saw myself wearing it in a dream. The next day, I culled the biggest feather out of a bag of feathers I had bought at a crafts store, held it up to my earlobe, and felt calm...right. Even so, I didn't consciously recognize the feather's symbolic nature for a while, though I wore it every day.

The earring was a compromise. My spirit was pushing to be set free, but I wasn't ready to reveal that part of my nature. The feather was a constant, private reminder of my spirit's need, and simultaneously a subtle, public declaration of my spirituality, revealed only to people who would hone in on the spiritual meaning. Those who didn't would get lost in the ambiguity and associate the symbolism with their own ideas. Mistaken interpretations would allow me to share my faith with the like-minded, while protecting myself from people who wouldn't understand.

Graduate school was the last place I expected to deepen and release my spiritual self, but that's when the feather lost resonance for me, and I stopped wearing it. Studying death, dying and the accompanying rites cannot be done honestly, I discovered, without one's spirit, without opening oneself to the bare bones of life and the essence of who we are. By the time I finished my Master's degree, even the silver butterfly necklace I'd worn for years for its transformation energy, broke. It no longer felt soothing, or *right* to wear it, so I never repaired it. Something in me had changed. The transformative energy the necklace helped me hold was no longer necessary.

Since then, I've worn no jewelry. I feel I've been stripped to my essence, and this core energy is what I'm to show and work from. Eventually, I suspect jewelry will carry neither needed nor detracting energy for me. Rings, earrings, and bracelets will be neutral objects I can wear strictly for aesthetic appeal if I choose. But for now, jewelry case glass simply reflects my knowing that the time is not right for adornment. Which, of course, doesn't stop my checking just to be sure.

Recently, I found my white feather in my jewelry box. I still liked the look, and remembered how comforting it felt when I wore it. *Hey, I should wear it again,* I thought. *Just occasionally.* But when I hung it on my ear, I sensed an adamant, "No. It's done."

Relationships, events, or patterns in my life—I realized that when they're over, they're over. The energy has been integrated, if I needed it for building or balancing, or dissipated if I needed to rid myself of that type of energy. Either way, no substantive connection or resonance exists to sustain the attraction or prolonged interaction.

I can get nostalgic every once in a while and rummage through my jewelry box or photo album, unearth diaries or my old sleeveless army-surplus jacket, e-mail a friend from college, or attend a high school reunion. But trying to hold on to something or someone when the energy is gone can feel empty or dead. Eventually the relationship may turn destructive, or shake free no matter how fiercely I cling.

Accepting impermanence and letting go when necessary is difficult with human relationships, especially family members. People can grow together, at a similar pace and path. When they do, the warm bonds of companionship buttress the stresses and strains of change.

But all too often, people settle in on their idea of who they are and who others are and defend this conceptual status quo by enforcing or reverting to expected behavior. I've seen capable, independent adults visit their parents and regress to infancy or resume adolescent battles. Some women, forceful and decisive on the job, wilt like the proverbial shrinking violet in their husband's presence. Conflict and potential abandonment looms if anyone in these relationships tries to grow. Unless change is imperative, it's easier to acquiesce.

Every major growth stage in my life has brought a new set of friends and colleagues. It's not that I threw away the previous relationships. In fact, initially I tried to maintain contact. But I soon learned it doesn't work, at least not on a long-term basis. In subtle ways, former friends let me know I was no longer one of them. They sidestepped my suggestions to go to old hangouts when I visited. Our conversations were stilted. Minor comments about my job, or clothes or living arrangements compared to the past revealed discomfort. Eventually invitations ceased, as did my attempts to e-mail or phone.

I had moved away in all respects.

Like material objects, some human relationships are meant to be momentary, or for a single purpose. Brenda, an e-mail acquaintance, realized this truth while praying in church. Standing next to a stranger, who was praying too, Brenda saw their prayer energy join forces and multiply. She felt a soul connection with this man. They were intentionally merging their energy, she sensed, and had done so in the past as brother and sister.

Ordinarily, after experiencing such a connection, Brenda would have tried to talk with the man, seek him out, and maybe establish an ongoing relationship. Instead, she felt a calm acceptance that following up wasn't necessary, that their connection in this life may be solely for that one instance of uniting in prayer.

Whether with material objects, natural objects, or human relationships, our attractions and interactions involve energy exchanges. Often, these exchanges are transient and minute enough to go unnoticed. But when an attraction is sustained, or when the object or relationship resonates deeply, recognizing and accepting the nature of the exchange can reveal truths that help us grow.

SEEING PATTERNS

WHEN OUR SPIRIT HAS AN IMPORTANT MESSAGE or insight for us, it will send the information repeatedly, in various forms, and for a lifetime if necessary. If we pay attention, we can see the patterns and understand the communication.

The first time I heard a message that I still periodically receive, I was seventeen and coaching a younger girls' softball team. We were ahead in the game and three or four of the team members were hanging over the dugout joking and talking with friends. Just as I yelled, "Hey you guys, get your head in the game," one of the girls' older sisters walked by and asked, "Don't you ever lighten up?"

"Don't you want to win the game?" I snapped.

She walked away but her comment stuck. These girls worked hard most of the time, we were winning, and yet I continued driving them, like I drove myself. Trying is what it's all about, I believed.

Pushing yourself. Staying focused. Persevering. This intensity and determination is a defining part of my personality that helps me overcome obstacles and achieve goals. But balance, I discovered, is crucial. Not everything in life requires relentless effort. Some things, such as spiritual insight or walled off talents, simply need to be allowed to emerge...to be.

Nearly twenty years later, when I was in my late thirties, I bought a new car. Three model years passed before I could decide what type of car to buy. When I finally made my choice, the car I wanted was at the end of its last production year. Most dealers were sold out. I HAD to find this vehicle.

I'm not usually interested in owning things, but occasionally there's an object I'm drawn toward, like my antique picture agate bracelet or silver butterfly necklace. When that happens, it's typically symbolic, or the object contains or attracts essential energy that's needed in my life. After I've integrated that energy, or that quality, the object is no longer necessary and leaves me. Often, it breaks, or I lose it. Especially if I try to hold onto it when its purpose is done. If I haven't developed that clingy ego attachment to it, then my interest in the object fades or I no longer find it attractive. It ends up in the closet, the trashcan, or someone else's house.

As I scrambled to find a black Honda Del Sol, I realized this car was one of those objects—the reason why I felt I HAD to have it. What your spirit needs, will manifest. Just trust it. Remembering that, I relaxed and found the car with my first phone call. On my way to the dealership, this car's symbolism and the type of energy fueling my choice emerged. Lightness. Play. Not taking life too seriously. It was soul food. The car would be a daily reminder to lighten up and enjoy life. To stop *trying* so hard.

But I'm stubborn. There's no denying it. Any story my family tells about my first five years of living confirms this personality trait. So it's no surprise that my spirit is forced to drive its point home again and again, in various ways, before my resistance finally cracks.

After three years of cruising around and playing in my Del Sol, I was perusing the shelves in a bookstore and opened a tiny book of aphorisms. Whatever page you turn to first, the introduction explained, is the message your soul is sending you. My fingers landed on a short verse about joy, fun, light-heartedness. Geez! This was no revelation. It was another reminder. *I know, I know,* I thought. *I'm trying to have fun.*

Living from spirit is as much about letting go and trusting the guidance as anything else. But I like running my own life, so I usually believe I know what I need. Often I drift to sleep with a question or topic in mind and wake up with some insight, answer, or direction. At times I consciously let myself drift when I'm working on a problem. In that light, dozing state, which an acquaintance calls "marinating," answers frequently arrive and I wake and record them. Sometimes, though, my spirit overrides my request and hands me something I didn't expect. Other issues, it decides, are more pressing.

One morning I woke up with the song "Yankee Doodle Dandy"

running through my head. Irritating. I went to sleep expecting to start the day with some wisdom to impart, some new insight about getting my publishing company off the ground, or adding to my book manuscript. Instead, this silly song was annoying me and I couldn't find the off button.

I got in my Del Sol to go to work, notepad on the seat beside me, just in case inspiration hit. Before I even backed out of the driveway, I heard the phrase, "Two Heavy Women." So I wrote it down. I didn't know what it referred to so I started *trying* to figure it out. A book title? A poem? A business name? I liked the double entendre. My partner and I are both, well...weighty, and the subject areas I write about—spirituality, transformation, and death and dying—are a bit heavy. But my company name was an intuition from years ago. I knew its purpose immediately and never doubted it. So what WAS this message?

Then I heard laughter, and laughed myself. Blinded by expectation, and still *trying*, still pushing toward *my* goal, I'd missed the "lighten up" reminders and their humorous delivery. Sometimes my spirit tricks me. It has to.

MAKING CONNECTIONS

I NEED A HEARING AID? Ironic. With only a 50% hearing capacity, the world's so noisy it makes me cringe. *Wax build-up*, I thought, when I made the audiologist appointment. A little solvent, a bit of swabbing, and I figured I'd be able to hear the board room voices again without straining, without reaching and stretching to grab the words before they get swallowed by the gray hum that muffles sentences and bites off word endings.

Instead, the audiologist hung a delicate beige quarter-moon over my right ear. "What's that whirring noise," I asked, shocked at my own voice. Loud and electronic, like voices crinkled and stretched by synthesizers.

"It's just the hearing aid's motor, " she said. "You'll get used to it. Your brain will filter it out like it does so much of the world's noise."

"It sounds tinny, electric, like everything's coming from a microphone."

"Well, it is an amplifying device," she says. I worry that I'll never hear the world naturally again. That birds will sound twangy instead of raucous or reedy. That I'll imagine humans as robots, their electronically distorted voices robbing me of connection to them. "You aren't hearing the world as it is *now*," she says.

"What's that humming?"

"The printer."

"That buzzing?"

"The air conditioner." She's smiling. I'm not. "Go outside, wander around awhile and hear what the world sounds like."

The door I'd entered from an ordinary parking lot an hour ago now opened into a pinball machine where church bells crashed, tires flapped against asphalt streets, electric wires sizzled, car doors banged, distant sirens squealed a block away. Even shoes made scuffing, scraping sounds against the concrete as pedestrians hurried by, oblivious to my sweating, shuddering, throbbing immersion in their world. Any minute I expected a big silver ball to roll over me, rattling and crunching, on its way home.

How the hell can anyone hear their inner voice in this screeching, screaming world? If our brain is busy filtering out all this junk, undoubtedly it tosses out the subtle messages whose medium is silence. The sounds it catches are the loudest, the most demanding, the most immediate. Our spirit shouts only when it has no other option.

My spirit shouts by using my body, the barometer of my inner state. Sometimes an illness is only physical. There are no deeper layers or meanings in it. But my hearing loss didn't feel one-dimensional. The obvious interpretation, that my ears were shutting down to force me to listen internally, didn't make sense. Nor did it sit right. I could hear my inner voice. It's nagged me for years to open myself to the world, so I was confused about why I was losing my hearing. Deafness is a sure way to be isolated from the mainstream. How can I open myself to the world if I can't hear it?

My job was one of those meant-to-be experiences and one of the mechanisms forcing me to be open to the world. Every detail just fell into place when I applied for it, and the work required me to listen carefully and interact with numerous people every day. Nope, this hearing loss made no sense. It took more than two years, and my conscious recognition of a recurring dream, before the message became clear.

I've dreamed this dream periodically for about a dozen years. I'm naked in public. Maybe I'm on a train, or in a restaurant, or walking down the sidewalk, in the raw. Nothing to it, as natural as the sun. Until somebody calls it to my attention and points out the inappropriateness.

When the dream first occurred, the pointing person had to get adamant, jumping and yelling at me and calling on others for reinforcement before I recognized my offense and acquiesced to their demand that I cover myself. I didn't understand the problem. But if it upset them that much, no sweat. They wanted me to put on clothes. I put on clothes.

Most recently, the person in my dream didn't even need to speak, just glanced my way and I cringed and scurried for cover, ashamed and chastising myself for not having known better. After all, no one wanted to see my nude body, even if I didn't mind them seeing it. I should comfort them and cover myself.

This time I woke up angry. Angry at the people doing the pointing for their fear, their scolding, their inability to let me be and to be themselves. And angry at me for allowing myself to run, to hide, to feel bad about showing my naturalness, showing who I am unadorned.

This time I understood that this dream was connected to my hearing loss. Instead of a contradiction, my body's shutting-out-the-world response and my spirit's simultaneously pushing me to open up were both part of the message. My spirit was prodding me to be open in the world, but was simultaneously warning me that I was listening too closely to external demands. Be in the world, it was telling me, but be who you are, unadorned.

NOCTURNAL TUNING

Dreams are a common communication pathway for spirit, perhaps because sleep is the one time most of us are still enough and defenseless enough to listen. With so much information to process, business to take care of, and psychological, emotional, and cultural baggage to carry around during waking hours, our spirit's voice rarely takes center stage.

In the quieter, calmer space of sleep, dreams can reveal our path and point to needed course corrections, actions we should take in our waking life. But I've learned recently, through dreams, that change doesn't always require conscious action when we're awake. Change can occur in other realms and simply manifest in wake life.

During my struggle to accept that it was time to speak publicly about spirituality, I experienced an unusual set of dreams. I think of these dreams as my nocturnal initiation or other-realm transformation.

On four consecutive nights, my dreams revolved around shifting foundations and new life. During each dream, I changed, not metaphorically, but literally. The change was not an awareness or action I thought about the next day and interpreted or implemented. I changed while I slept, during the dream state.

The first of these dreams grabbed my attention by its brevity and repetition. Usually my dreams are long and complex, but when I'm to remember a single point or take a specific action, my dreams are laser-focused. In this dream, a blue symbol repeated over and over along with the words "new beginnings."

Writing *Natural Urges,* I sensed, would open a new stage of my life and I woke feeling buoyant at this dream's confirmation of my knowing. I didn't understand, though, why I was compelled to draw the image and words in my bedside notebook. After twenty or so years of dream guidance, I rarely write dreams down anymore. If anything is significant, I usually know immediately. And if I do miss an important message, the dream eventually repeats. Besides, this image had burned itself into my consciousness. How could I forget?

At this point, I didn't realize the dream was the first step in my other-realm transformation process, nor did I connect all the dots until the dream series ended. After each dream, or transformation session, I felt the need to record the details. If I hadn't, I may not have noticed the progression.

In my dream the second night, I was sentenced to die. I didn't know who sentenced me, but I knew the verdict was official. Poison, wafer-like pills were mailed to me and I was to carry out my own execution. Friends and family members filled my house on the day I swallowed the tablets, but nobody cared. They milled around, talking, laughing, playing games, and paying scant attention when my body writhed or I complained about the injustice. After all, I'd committed no crimes, certainly nothing any worse than anyone else.

Since they wouldn't pay attention, I left. When I walked by a crowded softball field, I considered shouting my outrage from their PA system. But I knew no one in the bleachers or dugouts would care either. Then I realized I'd taken only one-and-one-quarter of the two wafers and wasn't going to die. I realized too that I had issued my own death sentence.

This dream echoed my wake-life resistance to the changes I needed to undergo to carry out my purpose on earth. I've known a transformation equivalent to death is required, yet fear has kept me chipping away at it rather than embracing or committing to my path. In the dream, everyone except me knew the choices were mine, so no one was going to give me any unwarranted sympathy.

I woke up feeling embarrassed and wimpy, but certain that I'd chosen my path. I no longer felt coerced, or sentenced by an external force. With no one to lash out against, my remaining battle was my own refusal to let go of aspects of myself that I no longer needed and would not serve me well, but that I still believed were necessary for my survival.

The next night, in another long, complicated dream, I drove onto the freeway ramp but realized this was the wrong path. I needed to stay on the side road. At the last moment I yanked the wheel to the right, shot across the dividing line, then stopped on a tree-covered plateau to determine my location, but found no map. When I walked to a nearby triplex to ask for directions, the building was deserted. I headed back to my car, but it was stolen. *I'll call my partner*, I thought, but my phone was not in my briefcase, so I started walking, hoping to find familiar streets.

After a few miles, I still didn't recognize the territory, so I decided to return the way I came. But when I turned around, the landscape changed. The streets and buildings I'd just passed did not exist. Taking that route anyway, the earth turned to water. Reddish brown waves covered everything, including me. I panicked; then realized I could swim. When I relaxed, a spot of ground appeared and I pulled myself onto it. I woke to the words, "You have stepped into your power."

Throughout the day, I felt strong, confident and mature. I had indeed moved into a new phase of life. I was committed to my path and knew that the resources I need are within me. The unknown, I learned in the dream, is nothing to fear and I can let go of the external tools that are no longer necessary to navigate.

The next night the clincher dream came. It began with a web site filled with information. Some phrases were visible to some people but not to others. The whole site was cloudy. Intermittently, I could read pieces of the writing, but not all of it.

I flew and floated through a series of scenes and experiences, mostly related to foundations and structures, accompanied by a non-human protector/teacher shaped like a blimp or a big cigar flying below me, like a pillow supporting me. A sidekick, a smaller version of the blimp, joined us in our sky sailing. At each scene, we hovered awhile to observe and discuss, or I joined in the scene taking various roles, then returned to my companions for a review to assure my understanding.

When the dream ended, I was leaving this experiential tour. As I stepped through the door, the whole web site of knowledge appeared clearly, neatly laid out in outline form for me to read. I woke accepting that I know what I need to know to fulfill my purpose and that answers are available when I need them.

This dream series, this other-realm transformation, gave me the peace and confidence to write this book and sealed my commitment to pursuing my purpose, whatever that brings. It also confirmed a lesson I'm learning in many other forms. We need not struggle over everything. Some things just *are*, if we'll simply let them be.

FEET ON THE GROUND

OPENING TO SPIRITUAL ENERGY can be a frightening experience to people who are not attempting to make the connection. We may be routinely going about our daily lives, then one day hear a disembodied voice, or find we are reading people's minds. Maybe we can ignore it, or write it off as a fluke—but not if the experience repeats. Others may find life crashing around them, divorce, illness, bankruptcy, and to top it off, a recurring dream, or a vision, or seeing details of settings they're not in and have never been in before. These unexpected connections or "openings" can make us fear we're going crazy.

To people engaged in a practice intended to heighten spiritual awareness, opening can be a heady experience. Feeling spiritual energy moving through us can produce an incredible high. This expansive feeling of oneness with all life can make us want to wrap our arms around the planet and dance for eternity. The exhilaration can become so intense, especially if the opening comes with an extraordinary experience like voices or visions or an out-of-body excursion, we might not even be able to function.

In this state, behavior can veer off track. Random thoughts or trivial events can mistakenly take on tremendous significance and include calls to action like digging up the backyard to find the door to the earth's center, or quitting a job in the certainty that winning the lottery is at hand. We can develop a messiah complex, believing we are receiving a "special" message. Or we believe we've been given knowledge no one else possesses, or that we single-handedly must save the world. Not only are we obnoxious at this point, messages received in this frame of mind likely will be distorted or useless. Even if the insight is a truth, we probably can't boil the message down succinctly enough to understand or communicate it in words. Our entire awareness of and connection with the universe and its power can't be brought to the physical plane in one piece.

It's easy to fear or get enthralled with spiritual communication and let our feet slip off the ground. Navigating the spiritual world in the physical requires firm roots in the earth. Spiritual energy is inside and all around us. We are its grounding. We are the conduit through which spirit can affect the material world.

Being in the world, grounded in the physical, is where we learn the earth's spiritual lessons. Compassion, for example, is an earth plane teaching. It won't be learned by getting lost in Buddha bliss. We learn compassion by opening ourselves to suffering, that of others and our own. By sitting with the real, tangible tears and pain of friends, family, and strangers. By facing the experience head on, not trying to look away or soften it into something less than it is, something unreal and easier to bear. Forgetting our physical nature will take us down the wrong road.

Opening up to the spirit realm and its ways of knowing can get confusing. We can find ourselves in a muddle, bombarded by disparate and random bits of information, or receiving just enough snippets to let us know something's up, without revealing the whole picture. In my frustration, I've demanded, "Just tell me what it is and what I'm to do!" But the universe, I've found, seldom accedes to demands. Knowing is revealed in its own time. Relinquishing expectations and the need for control can relieve anxiety and help spiritual energy flow.

For some of us, the energy starts flowing and no regulatory valve is in sight. We may receive a huge amount of information, usually with no idea what to do with it or how to interpret it. Not all of the energy flying around is intended for us. Over time, we learn to distinguish, but at the beginning of a new awakening, the wide-open receptivity can pick up everything within its range. This constant flow can become draining and disturbing.

To work with spirit's energies without being consumed or overwhelmed, we need to learn to modulate the flow. Balance is key. Spiritual energy is not to be attended to constantly. We are not puppets waiting for spirit to direct our next move. Yet when the awakening experience is new, it can be fascinating. What will happen next? What does it mean? What is it? Where is it coming from? Reluctance to pull oneself away from the energy is a common response. Eventually, though, we reach overload. Then the desire to shut down or moderate the flow kicks in.

Taking care of physical needs is one way to bring balance to a spiritual awakening. Eating regularly, sleeping regularly, cleaning the house, weeding the garden, and tending to one's family or job are patterns and tasks that often go by the wayside if we become preoccupied with the spiritual realm. Re-engaging in these activities can bring grounding without completely blocking spiritual energy. Once spirit has our attention, it won't permanently go away.

Suspending participation in awakening exercises or meditations is another balancing necessity at times. The same goes for reading, listening to tapes, or watching videos about spirituality. These practices are designed to facilitate spiritual opening. After we're open, both the process and our needs change. At that point it's about listening, distinguishing, and learning to live with our feet on the ground and a consistent connection to our spirit.

MANY THANKS

To Nancy Fenn, Rhea White,
and Gloria Oelman for their encouragement
in the early drafts of this manuscript.
To Susan Browne for her editorial
suggestions, and to my partner,
Jul Lowery, for editing, proofreading,
and sharing life with me.

ORDER FORM

Twisted Tree Press
P. O. Box 17816
Seattle, WA 98107
www.twistedtreepress.com
info@twistedtreepress.com
(206) 999-7518

Send To: (Information will not be sold or provided to any other organization.)

NAME _____

STREET ADDRESS _____

CITY/STATE/ZIP _____

PHONE (____) _____ COUNTRY _____

EMAIL _____

Payment:

Natural Urges (ISBN 0-9717950-0-2)		$15.00 US ($23 CAN)
	QUANTITY	_____
	SUBTOTAL	$ _____
add 8.8% to orders shipped to WA state	SALES TAX	$ _____
For shipping (U.S.): $5 first book & $1.50 each additional book **International:** $9 first book & $3 each additional book	SHIPPING	$ _____
	TOTAL	$ _____

Please make check or money order payable
to **Twisted Tree Press**
Thank you!